P9-CFV-988

100
WORDS
TO MAKE YOU
SOUND
SMART

THE **100 WORDS**® *From the Editors of the*
AMERICAN HERITAGE®
DICTIONARIES

HOUGHTON MIFFLIN HARCOURT
Boston   New York

THE 100 WORDS® is a registered trademark of Houghton Mifflin Harcourt.

Visit our websites: hmhbooks.com
and ahdictionary.com

LIBRARY OF CONGRESS CATALOGING-IN-PUBLICATION DATA

100 words to make you sound smart / from the editors of the American Heritage dictionaries.
   p. cm. -- (100 words)
 ISBN-13: 978-0-618-71488-9
 ISBN-10: 0-618-71488-X
 1. Vocabulary. 2. English language--Etymology. I. Title: One hundred words to make you sound smart.
 PE1449.A147 2006
 422--dc22

2006018817

Text design by Anne Chalmers

MANUFACTURED IN THE UNITED STATES OF AMERICA

16 17 18 - DOC - 15 14 13

Table of Contents

Preface

Like its predecessors in our popular 100 Words series, *100 Words to Make You Sound Smart* is a handy treasury of words that have been handpicked by the editors of the American Heritage® dictionaries. This highly informative and entertaining book, the sixth in the series, offers words that can imbue everyday conversation with exceptional precision and eloquence.

The words in this book have been carefully chosen because each conveys a specific meaning in a way that enlivens everyday speaking and writing. Just as a single picture can often be an efficient substitute for many sentences of text, each of the 100 words, such as *finagle, cloying,* and *epitome,* is concisely and colorfully expressive. These words are not technical or obscure, nor are they pompous or intimidating. Rather, they are extraordinarily effective in ordinary situations.

While many people are familiar with these words and will have encountered them in their reading, they may not know how to incorporate them into conversation. We have therefore chosen nearly 200 passages from magazines, books, newspapers, movies, TV shows, and speeches that show how the words have been used by contemporary and historical speakers and writers. These quotations are intended to illustrate clearly how the selected words can enhance communication in almost any setting—in the workplace, at home, or among friends.

The richness and variety of English is reflected in this engaging selection that is also eminently useful. These words come from popular culture (*Catch-22*) and from classical antiquity (*spartan, stoic*). There are words named after famous people (*Freudian slip, Machiavellian*), words borrowed from other languages (*carte blanche, kitsch*), words that have multiple syllables (*equivocate, quintessential*), and words that have only one (*glib, waft*). Words with interesting histories are discussed further in detailed notes that describe how their meanings have developed over time.

Language is nothing less than an essential conduit for our most intriguing ideas, cherished hopes, and powerful passions. We hope that these words will help readers to explain, to persuade, and even to enchant as they pursue the worthy endeavor of self-expression.

—Susan Spitz,
Senior Editor

Guide to the Entries

ENTRY WORDS The 100 words in this book are listed alphabetically. The pronunciation of the word follows the entry word (see page ix for a pronunciation key). At least one part of speech follows each entry word. All entry words are clearly defined. Some entries have more than one sense, or meaning. Multiple senses are numbered.

QUOTATIONS Each definition is followed by quotations from speeches, books, films, articles, or other sources to show the word's usage. In each case, the author or speaker, the title of the source, and its date are indicated. The order of the quotations corresponds to the order of senses presented. The quotations were chosen to encompass a wide spectrum of ideas and beliefs expressed by a diverse group of speakers and authors.

ETYMOLOGIES (WORD HISTORIES) Most words have etymologies that appear in square brackets following the quotations. An etymology traces the history of a word as far back in time as can be determined with reasonable certainty. The stage most closely preceding Modern English is given first, with each earlier stage following in sequence. A language name, linguistic form (in italics), and brief definition of the form are given for each stage of the derivation. To avoid redundancy, a language or definition is not repeated if it is identical to the corresponding item in the immediately preceding stage. Occasionally, a form will be given that is not actually preserved in written documents but which scholars are confident did exist; such a form will be marked by an asterisk (*). The word *from* is used to indicate origin of any kind: by inheritance, borrowing, or derivation. When an etymology splits a compound word into parts, a colon introduces the parts and each element is then traced back to its origin, with those elements enclosed in parentheses.

NOTES   Some entries include notes that present additional interesting information regarding the history of the word, including the process by which it entered English from other languages. These notes discuss the historical, cultural, or literary origins of the word and ways that it is used in addition to the senses that have been presented. Some compound words have word history notes instead of explicit etymologies.

Pronunciation Guide

Pronunciations appear in parentheses after boldface entry words. If a word has more than one pronunciation, the first pronunciation is usually more common than the other, but often they are equally common. Pronunciations are shown after inflections and related words where necessary.

Stress is the relative degree of emphasis that a word's syllables are spoken with. An unmarked syllable has the weakest stress in the word. The strongest, or primary, stress is indicated with a bold mark (ʹ). A lighter mark (ʹ) indicates a secondary level of stress. The stress mark follows the syllable it applies to. Words of one syllable have no stress mark because there is no other stress level that the syllable can be compared to.

The key on page ix shows the pronunciation symbols used in this book. To the right of the symbols are words that show how the symbols are pronounced. The letters whose sound corresponds to the symbols are shown in boldface.

The symbol (ə) is called *schwa*. It represents a vowel with the weakest level of stress in a word. The schwa sound varies slightly according to the vowel it represents or the sounds around it:

abundant (ə-bŭnʹdənt)   **moment** (mōʹmənt)

civil (sĭvʹəl)   **grateful** (grātʹfəl)

PRONUNCIATION KEY

Symbol	Examples	Symbol	Examples
ă	pat	oi	noise
ā	pay	ŏŏ	took
âr	care	ŏŏr	lure
ä	father	ōō	boot
b	bib	ou	out
ch	church	p	pop
d	deed, milled	r	roar
ĕ	pet	s	sauce
ē	bee	sh	ship, dish
f	fife, phase, rough	t	tight, stopped
		th	thin
g	gag	*th*	this
h	hat	ŭ	cut
hw	which	ûr	urge, term, firm, word, heard
ĭ	pit		
ī	pie, by		
îr	deer, pier	v	valve
j	judge	w	with
k	kick, cat, pique	y	yes
l	lid, needle	z	zebra, xylem
m	mum	zh	vision, pleasure, garage
n	no, sudden		
ng	thing	ə	about, item, edible, gallop, circus
ŏ	pot		
ō	toe		
ô	caught, paw		
ôr	core	ər	butter

Jimmy was making a real meal of it, head down, fingers thumping, and at the last crashing chord, he held up one hand in a flourish a foot above the keyboard before letting it fall by his side in the true manner of the concert pianist.

I doubt if the Methodist Hall has ever heard a noise like the great cheer which followed. The place erupted in a storm of clapping and shouting, and Jimmy was not the man to ignore such an **accolade**.

— James Herriot,
The Lord God Made Them All, 1981

accolade (ăk'ə-lād' *or* ăk'ə-läd')

noun

1. An expression of approval. **2.** A special acknowledgment, such as an award.

> There's also a funny thing when an actor retires and reaches his sixties. Awards and **accolades** start chasing you around. Sometimes they give them to you just so that you'll attend the dinner and they can sell tickets, but usually they are on the up-and-up.
>
> — Maureen O'Hara, *'Tis Herself,* 2004

[From French, *accolade,* an embrace, accolade, from *accoler,* to embrace, from Old French *acoler,* from Vulgar Latin *accollāre : Latin *ad-*, to, toward + Latin *collum,* neck.]

> In tracing *accolade* back to its Latin origins, we find that it was formed from the prefix *ad-*, "to, toward," and the noun *collum*, "neck," which may bring the word *collar* to mind. From these elements came the Vulgar Latin word *accollāre, which was the source of French *accolade*, "an embrace." An embrace was originally given to a knight when dubbing him, which is why *accolade* traditionally refers to the ceremonial bestowal of knighthood.

acrimony (ăk′rə-mō′nē)

noun

Bitter, sharp hostility, especially in speech.

> Some conversations I have heard in our own country sound like old records, long-playing, left over from the middle thirties. The debate of the thirties had its great significance and produced great results, but it took place in a different world with different needs and different tasks. It is our responsibility today to live in our own world and to identify the needs and discharge the tasks of the 1960s. If there's any current trend towards meeting present problems with old clichés, this is the moment to stop it — before it lands us all in a bog of sterile **acrimony**.
>
> — President John F. Kennedy, Yale University Commencement Address, June 11, 1962

> **Acrimony** so intense, so uncompromising, so vicious, so unhealthy underscores the one tenet of the fan canon that is absolutely biblical in its inflexibility: *Never forgive, never forget.*
>
> — Joe Queenan, *True Believers: The Tragic Inner Life of Sports Fans*, 2003

[From Latin *ācrimōnia*, sharpness, from *ācer*, sharp.]

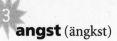

angst (ängkst)

noun

A feeling of anxiety or apprehension.

> Organizing high school students is extremely difficult. Apart from being an impermanent base (students graduate), they are inexperienced and often politically uninformed.... Their disconnectedness and isolation — easily caricatured as pouty alienation or **angst** — are rooted in the realities of their lives: their lack of mobility, frequent lack of access to people who share their concerns and passions, and relative lack of personal and political power.
>
> — Liza Featherstone, "Hot-Wiring High School," *The Nation*, June 21, 1999

> I was . . . miserable in the very tributaries of my soul; I cried to myself, feeling an **angst** of such intense sorrow that to this day the remembered pain comes back to me as a beastly predator.
>
> — Willie Morris, *Taps*, 2001

[From German *Angst*, from Middle High German *angest*, from Old High German *angust*.]

anomaly (ə-nŏm′ə-lē)

noun

Someone or something that deviates from the normal or common form, order, or rule; a peculiarity or abnormality.

> Goalies back then also played most of their careers without masks. Standing up reduced the chances of injury, from both pucks and sticks. Glenn Hall . . . introduced the butterfly technique, fanning his legs out in a V to cover the lower corners. But Hall didn't remain on the ice. He was up as quickly as he went down, and both he and his butterfly were viewed as **anomalies**, not to be copied by youngsters.
>
> — E.M. Swift, "Seems Like Old Times," *Sports Illustrated*, February 20, 1995

> The two nuns on either side of me sang the plaintive Arabic hymns off-key, which made the beautiful songs sound even sadder. The nuns were all short and olive-skinned, with heavy, dark brows. I was an **anomaly**, yet no one looked curiously at me. In fact, nobody seemed to notice me at all, which pleased me.
>
> — Rosemary Mahoney, *The Singular Pilgrim: Travels on Sacred Ground*, 2003

[From Late Latin *anōmalia*, from Greek *anōmaliā*, unevenness, irregularity, from *anōmalos*, uneven, irregular, probably from *an-*, not + *homalos*, even (from *homos*, same).]

antidote (ăn′tĭ-dōt′)

noun

An agent that counteracts something that is poisonous or otherwise harmful.

> I believe the best **antidote** to vulgarity and brutality is the power of a better example, of love over indifference.
>
> — Vice President Al Gore, Columbine Memorial Address, April 25, 1999

> We've got to teach history and nurture history and encourage history because it's an **antidote** to the hubris of the present — the idea that everything we have and everything we do and everything we think is the ultimate, the best.
>
> — David McCullough, "Knowing History and Knowing Who We Are," speech given at Hillsdale College, February 15, 2005

[From Middle English *antidote,* from Latin *antidotum,* from Greek *antidoton,* from *antididonai, antido-,* to give as a remedy against : *anti-,* against, in opposition to + *didonai,* to give.]

avant-garde (ä'vänt-gärd' *or* ăv'änt-gärd')

noun

A group that creates or promotes innovative or unconventional ideas in a given field, especially the arts.

adjective

Relating to such a group.

> *The youth* was a favorite topic in 1968. Riots broke out on the campuses as the antiwar movement reached its peak.... The press seemed to enjoy presenting these youths as the **avant-garde** who were sweeping aside the politics and morals of the past and shaping America's future.
>
> — Tom Wolfe, *Hooking Up*, 2000

> The **avant-garde** aroused in Hitler only incomprehension and revulsion. His own practice of art was limited to painstaking, lifeless reproductions of buildings; his own taste in art never moved beyond the kind of conventional, classically inspired representations that were the stock-in-trade of the Academy that he had so wanted to join in Vienna.
>
> — Richard J. Evans, *The Coming of the Third Reich*, 2003

> Jaramil looked at the face of the girl with glasses, and his heart was wrung by the thought that he might lose her.... He had not yet shown her his poems; the painter had promised to have them published in an **avant-garde** magazine, and he counted on the prestige of the printed word to dazzle the girl.
>
> — Milan Kundera, *Life Is Elsewhere*, 1973

[From French *avant-garde*, vanguard, from Old French : *avant*, before (from Latin *abante*, in front : *ab*, from + *ante*, before) + *garde*, guard (of Germanic origin).]

baroque (bə-rōk′)

adjective

Extravagant, complex, or bizarre, especially in ornamentation.

> Although this masked vigilante [Spider-Man] soon takes up residence on the front page of the city's tabloids, his most **baroque** entanglement is the long-running masochistic charade with the girl next door.
>
> — J. Hoberman, "Almost Heroes," *Village Voice*, May 1–7, 2002

> I decided to start by reading Loyola's original *Spiritual Exercises* and some of the commentaries on them for myself. . . . I had hardly begun when I almost immediately gave up the effort. Both the *Exercises* and the commentaries, even in recent translations, are written in such **baroque** theological language that they lost me almost completely.
>
> — Harvey Cox, *When Jesus Came to Harvard*, 2004

[From French *baroque*, from Italian *barocco*, and from Portuguese *barroco*, imperfect pearl.]

> The word *baroque* also refers to a style in art, architecture, and music that flourished in Europe from about 1600 to 1750 and was characterized by elaborate ornamentation. It ultimately derives from Portuguese *barroco*, "irregularly shaped pearl." French borrowed this word as *baroque* and used it of baroque architecture, whose florid curves resemble the bumps, twists, and folds of such pearls. The French word, borrowed into English in the 1700s, may have been influenced by Medieval Latin *baroco*, a term coined by medieval philosophers to refer to an involved kind of logical argumentation. Writers of the Renaissance used *baroco* to mock those who clung to needlessly complicated medieval ideas.

bona fide (bō′nə fīd′ *or* bŏn′ə fīd′)

adjective

1. Made or carried out in good faith; sincere. **2.** Authentic; genuine.

> KENICKIE: I'll make an honest woman of you.
> RIZZO: If this is a line, I ain't biting.
> KENICKIE: That's a **bona fide** offer.
> RIZZO: Well, it ain't moonlight and roses, but . . .
>
> — from the film *Grease*, 1978

> My brother and I were huddled up beside them, hoping our mother would shut up and that the easy-talking guide with the pointy face and the short legs would be hired for the duration.
>
> "What do you want?" my father said, turning to Sandy and me.
>
> "Well, if it costs too much . . ." Sandy began.
>
> "Forget the cost," my father replied. "Do you like this guy or not?"
>
> "He's a character, Dad," Sandy whispered. "He looks like one of those duck decoys. I like when he says 'to be exact.'"
>
> "Bess," my father said, "the man is a **bona fide** guide to Washington, D.C. Don't believe he's ever cracked a smile but he's an alert little guy and he couldn't be more polite. Let me see if he'll take seven bucks."
>
> — Philip Roth, *The Plot Against America*, 2004

[From Latin *bonā fidē*, in good faith : *bonā*, feminine singular ablative form of *bonus*, good + *fidē*, ablative form of *fidēs*, faith.]

9

boondoggle (bo͞on′dô-gǝl)

noun

An unnecessary or wasteful activity.

> **MICHELE NORRIS:** Taller than the Brooklyn Bridge and almost as long as the Golden Gate, the Ralph M. Bartholomew Veterans' Memorial Bridge will get $223 million in the transportation bill. It will link the small port town of Ketchikan, Alaska, to nearby Gravina Island and its airport. . . .
>
> **MARY KAUFFMAN:** Well, the primary reason that you hear for people wanting the bridge is so that Ketchikan can expand. Ketchikan's located on an island. It's very mountainous, and so the city's spread out along the coastline. And by being able to move over to Gravina, the thought is that you could build and expand the city more and have more businesses.
>
> **MICHELE NORRIS:** Now those who are against the bridge, they call this a **boondoggle**.
>
> **MARY KAUFFMAN:** Right, the bridge to nowhere, the **boondoggle** bridge.
>
> —National Public Radio, *All Things Considered*,
> August 10, 2005

[Coined by Robert H. Link, American scoutmaster, originally in reference to a braided leather cord made and worn as a decoration by Boy Scouts.]

bourgeois (boŏr-zhwä′)

adjective

Relating to or typical of the middle class, especially in espousing respectability and conventional middle-class materialistic values.

> GUNNER: After all, why shouldn't she do it? The Russian students do it. Women should be as free as men. I'm a fool. I'm so full of your **bourgeois** morality that I let myself be shocked by the application of my own revolutionary principles. If she likes the man, why shouldn't she tell him so?
>
> — George Bernard Shaw, *Misalliance*, 1910

[From French *bourgeois*, from Old French *burgeis*, citizen of a town, from *bourg*, fortified town, from Late Latin *burgus*, fortress, of Germanic origin.]

RINGO: Leave them drums alone.

FLOOR MANAGER: Oh, surely one can have a tiny touch. I can just have a little touch.

RINGO: If you so much as breathe heavy on 'em, I'm out on strike.

FLOOR MANAGER: Aren't you being rather arbitrary?

RINGO: There you go hiding behind a smoke screen of **bourgeois** clichés. I don't go round messing about with your earphones, do I?

— from the film *A Hard Day's Night*, 1964

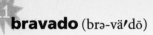

bravado (brə-vä′dō)

noun

A show of bravery or defiance, often intended to make an impression or mislead someone.

> **NARRATOR:** [upon hearing the *War of the Worlds* radio address] Despite his **bravado** all evening, Mr. Manulis panicked and bolted out of the car. He was so frightened by the reports of interplanetary invasion that he ran off, leaving Aunt Bea to contend with the slimy green monsters he expected to drop from the sky at any moment. She walked home six miles. When Mr. Manulis called her for a date the next week, she told my mother to tell him she couldn't see him anymore. She had married a Martian.
>
> — from the film *Radio Days*, 1987

The arrival of tractors and combines eliminated most field hands. The sharecropper became expendable, and as marginal farmers moved on, many towns and villages languished or disappeared entirely. That could have been Tulsa's fate. Instead, it became one of the most remarkable boomtowns in American history, and it did so with a can-do **bravado** and a shameless boosterism that shaped its self-image for the rest of the century.

— James S. Hirsch, *Riot and Remembrance*, 2002

[From French *bravade* and Old Spanish *bravada*, swagger, bravery, both ultimately from Vulgar Latin **brabus*, brave, from Latin *barbarus*, foreign, barbarous, from Greek *barbaros*, non-Greek, barbarous (imitative of the sound of unintelligible speech).]

brogue (brōg)

noun

A strong dialectal accent, especially a strong Irish or Scottish accent in English.

> THE NOTE TAKER: Simply phonetics. The science of speech. That's my profession: also my hobby. Happy is the man who can make a living by his hobby! You can spot an Irishman or a Yorkshireman by his **brogue**. I can place any man within six miles. I can place him within two miles in London. Sometimes within two streets.
>
> — George Bernard Shaw, *Pygmalion*, 1913

> It's time for St. Patrick's Day, time for the parade down the famous Avenue of the Astors and the Rockefellers. California is far from the great Irish cities of the East Coast. But I might as well have grown up in Boston or New York, so familiar was I as a boy with Ireland. Raised by Irish nuns and priests, I first heard English and Latin through their **brogue**. I grew up with kids with Irish faces, freckles, skin that flared red in the California sun.
>
> — Richard Rodriguez, from the TV show *The MacNeil/Lehrer NewsHour*, March 17, 1995

[Probably from *brogue,* heavy shoe of untanned leather worn by the Irish and Scottish peasantry (from a notion likening speech with a heavy Irish or Scottish accent to the wearing of brogues), from Irish *bróg* and Scottish Gaelic *bròg,* shoe, from Old Irish *bróc.*]

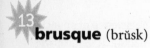

brusque (brŭsk)

adjective

Abrupt and curt in manner or speech; discourteously blunt.

> All week long SS bigwigs have been stomping through the puddles in the ice-cold raw cement structure, down in the enormous underground chambers and up above at the untried furnaces, their impatient **brusque** comments echoing to the splash and thump of boots.

> — Herman Wouk, *War and Remembrance*, 1978

[From French *brusque*, lively, fierce, from Italian *brusco*, coarse, rough, from Late Latin *brūscum*, perhaps blend of Late Latin *brūcus*, heather (of Celtic origin) and Latin *rūscus*, the plant known as butcher's broom or box holly (since both heather and butcher's broom are rough and can be used for making brooms).]

Strangers had a way of listening to his sales talk about the *Journal's* easy-to-read type with amused smiles and then saying, "No thank you." One man interrupted with a **brusque** "Not today" and closed the door in Henry's face. A lady embarrassed him by telling him what a splendid little salesman he was and then saying she couldn't afford to take another paper.

— Beverly Cleary,
  Henry and the Clubhouse,
  1962

byzantine *also* Byzantine

(bĭz'ən-tēn' *or* bĭz'ən-tīn')

adjective

Highly complicated; intricate and involved.

> The Professional Boxing Safety Act ensures that all boxing events in the US are approved and supervised by state athletic officials; medical services and insurance are provided to all boxers; and a nationwide system of boxer identification and suspension enforcement has been established. However, little appears to have changed regarding the business side of boxing. Professional boxing remains a secretive and inexplicable mix of private deal-making, **byzantine** ratings systems, and restrictive contracting practices. If professional boxing is ever to become the truly great and honorable sport it deserves to be, these areas must be reformed.
>
> — Senator John McCain, Senate testimony,
>   March 24, 1998

> The United States, with its 35-percent corporate income tax and its **byzantine** rules for taxing worldwide profits, is not a particularly friendly tax environment, especially compared with Bermuda, where there is no corporate income tax.
>
> — Jonathan Weisman, "A Question of Patriotism,"
>   *Washington Post*, September 28, 2002

[From Late Latin *Byzantīnus*, of the city of Byzantium, from *Byzantium*, Byzantium, from Greek *Byzantion*.]

The modern city now known as *Istanbul* has gone by many names over the centuries. It was founded by the Greeks in 667 BC as *Bȳzantion,* a name which the Romans later adapted into Latin as *Bȳzantium.* Byzantium occupied a strategic harbor on the Bosporus, a narrow strait connecting the Black Sea to the Sea of Marmara, and in 324 AD, the Roman emperor Constantine I made it the capital of the Eastern Roman Empire and renamed it *Nova Roma,* "New Rome." In the emperor's honor, the city came to be called "Constantine's city," or *Kōnstantinoupolis* in Greek, the source of the English name *Constantinople.*

After the disintegration of the Western Roman Empire, the Eastern Roman Empire evolved into the Byzantine Empire, whose designation is derived from the original name of its capital city. The Byzantine Empire was renowned for its cultural splendor and magnificent architecture, and the word *Byzantine* is used in English to describe the typical architectural style of Byzantine churches and other buildings, which were often characterized by a central dome resting on a cube formed by four round arches and by the extensive use of surface decoration such as veined marble panels, low relief carving, and colored glass mosaics. The Byzantine imperial government was notorious for its inflexible hierarchies, complicated politics, and palace intrigues, and this helped lead to the application of the English adjective *byzantine* to procedures or institutions that are intricate or overly complicated.

Byzantine politics came to an end in 1453, when the city fell to the Turks and became the capital of the Ottoman Empire, and in the 20th century, the official name of the Turkish city was changed to *Istanbul.*

cacophony (kə-kŏf′ə-nē)

noun

Jarring, discordant sound.

> There has been a sea change on oral argument over the last twenty years. In the eighties, there were three or four Justices who were content to sit back and let the advocate make his argument. Now it's like eight professors who all think they're going to ask the question that probes the deepest. They don't care about the architecture of an argument; they go straight to the issue they care about. They're using the lawyers as postmen to carry messages down the bench, and the result is often **cacophony**.
>
> — A.E. Dick Howard, professor of law, University of Virginia, quoted in Margaret Talbot, "Supreme Confidence," *The New Yorker*, March 28, 2005

> Just as the strength of the Internet is chaos, the strength of our liberty depends upon the chaos and **cacophony** of the unfettered speech the First Amendment protects.
>
> — Stewart Dalzell, circuit court judge, *ACLU v. Reno*, June 12, 1996

[From French *cacophonie*, from Greek *kakophōniā*, from *kakophōnos*, cacophonous : *kakos*, bad + *phōnē*, sound.]

camaraderie (kä′mə-rä′də-rē)

noun

Goodwill and lighthearted rapport between or among friends; comradeship.

> Small talk is crucial to maintain a sense of **camaraderie** when there is nothing special to say. Women friends and relatives keep the conversational mechanisms in working order by talking about small things as well as large. Knowing they will have such conversations later makes women feel they are not alone in life.
>
> — Deborah Tannen, *You Just Don't Understand*, 1990

> There is nothing like the team togetherness and **camaraderie** after a win. It's awesome. It's a rush, a blast. The place where it's most noticeable is in the locker room. I love being around the guys after a big win, the locker room celebrations. And I love flying home with the guys afterwards. Every now and then I'll force a little **camaraderie** because I feel it promotes teamwork. That's why I'll call off a practice and take everyone to a movie or go bowling.
>
> — Jon Gruden, quoted in Bob LaMonte, *Winning the NFL Way*, 2002

[From French *camaraderie*, from *camarade*, comrade, from Old French, roommate, from Old Spanish *camarada*, barracks company, roommate, from *cámara*, room, from Late Latin *camera*, from Latin, vault, from Greek *kamarā*.]

capricious (kə-prĭsh′əs or kə-prē′shəs)

adjective

Characterized by or subject to whim; impulsive and unpredictable.

> Many of the empire's failures lay in the man himself. Half-educated — able to read, but not to write — Charlemagne was vulgar and easily flattered. He was also **capricious**, at times pardoning his enemies, but on one occasion decapitating 4,500 surrendering Saxons. Though he loved making laws, few survived him.
>
> — "Castles of Sand: The Holy Roman Emperor,"
> *The Economist*, September 16, 2004

> In Taiwan . . . political dissidents won early support by helping citizens take on local authorities over pollution and environmental issues. Once Chinese begin to think of the legal system as something that works for them rather than a mystifying and **capricious** beast, authorities will have a harder and harder time holding themselves above the law.
>
> — Melinda Liu and Lijia Macleod, "Barefoot Lawyers," *Newsweek*, March 4, 2002

[From French *capricieux*, from Italian *capriccioso*, from *capriccio*, sudden start, fright : *capo*, head (from Latin *caput*) + *riccio*, curly (from Latin *ēricius*, hedgehog, since in a state of fright one's hair stands on end like the spines of a hedgehog).]

carte blanche (kärt blänsh′ *or* kärt blănsh′)

noun

Unrestricted power to act at one's own discretion; unconditional authority.

> GEORGE [*To Andy Kaufman*]: Listen, I got this job that I want you to take. It's guest-hosting the TV show "Fridays." It's not a great TV show, but it will be good for you. It's live, they'll give you **carte blanche**, and you'll get back in the business of making people laugh.
>
> — from the film *Man on the Moon*, 1999

> It may seem odd to let people claim rights under the very Constitution that they are trying to subvert. But bitter experience has shown us that the power to punish such bad speakers often ends up being used to punish good ones, too. Likewise, it might seem reasonable to provide less Fourth Amendment protection when the government is investigating really serious crimes, like murder. Why not give the police **carte blanche**, for instance, to search murder scenes?
>
> — Eugene Volokh, "The Fourth Amendment Meets the War on Terror," http://www.slate.com, June 17, 2002

[From French *carte blanche* : *carte,* ticket (from Latin *charta,* sheet of papyrus paper, from Greek *khartēs*) + *blanche,* feminine singular of *blanc,* white, blank (from Old French, of Germanic origin).]

Catch-22 *also* catch-22 (kăch′twĕn-tē-tōo′)

noun

A situation in which a desired outcome or solution is impossible to attain because of a set of inherently contradictory rules or conditions.

> I fully understand the **Catch-22** with getting an agent: Agents want someone who's published before, but how can a person get published without an agent? As hard as it is, it happens all the time. All successful writers were once in the same boat you are, but they found a way to do it.
>
> — Nicholas Sparks, "Three Steps in Becoming a Successful Author,"
> http://www.nicholassparks.com/WritersCorner/Success.html, 2002

> What is amazing about this story is how little nurses have benefited from their technological mastery. Sandelowski shrewdly diagnoses a classic **Catch-22**. While it is true that nurses' status is somewhat enhanced by their technical proficiency, the recognition they receive does not match their actual accomplishments. That's because physicians quickly label the technical activities nurses engage in as "simple enough" for a nurse to perform.
>
> — Suzanne Gordon, "Following Doctors' Orders,"
> *The Nation*, March 4, 2002

[After *Catch-22*, a novel by Joseph Heller (1923–1999), American writer.]

The popular catch phrase *Catch-22* was invented by Joseph Heller in his 1955 novel, *Catch-22*, which takes place in Italy during World War II. The main character, Captain Yossarian of the US Army Air Forces, and his fellow airmen have been ordered to fly ever-increasing numbers of dangerous missions. Looking for a way to avoid being killed, Yossarian asks if it is possible for a pilot—like his buddy Orr, for instance—to be grounded for reasons of insanity. The doctor at Yossarian's base explains that it *is* possible—in theory:

> There was only one catch and that was Catch-22, which specified that a concern for one's own safety in the face of dangers that were real and immediate was the process of a rational mind. Orr was crazy and could be grounded. All he had to do was ask; and as soon as he did, he would no longer be crazy and would have to fly more missions. Orr would be crazy to fly more missions and sane if he didn't, but if he was sane he had to fly them. If he flew them he was crazy and didn't have to; but if he didn't want to he was sane and had to.

The mysterious Catch-22, however, does not just simply cover relief from duties on grounds of insanity; throughout the novel, it manifests itself as the catch-all justification offered by the authorities for the most absurd and self-serving actions. As one character puts it: *Catch-22 says they have a right to do anything we can't stop them from doing.*

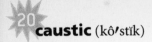

caustic (kô′stĭk)

adjective

Incisively critical or sarcastic; cutting.

> The satirist who writes nothing but satire should write but little — or it will seem that his satire springs rather from his own **caustic** nature than from the sins of the world in which he lives.
>
> — Anthony Trollope, *Autobiography of Anthony Trollope*, 1883

> To have the great Mme de Luxembourg in his thrall was a remarkable development, and Diderot and Grimm had reason to be jealous. In her youth she was exceptionally beautiful and also exceptionally independent, with an ability to wither admirers with **caustic** epigrams.
>
> — Leo Damrosch, *Jean-Jacques Rousseau*, 2005

[From Middle English *caustik*, from Latin *causticus*, from Greek *kaustikos*, from *kaustos*, red hot, from *kaiein*, *kau-*, to burn.]

A caustic substance is one that can burn, corrode, or dissolve something by chemical action. Most inorganic acids, such as sulfuric acid, are highly caustic. Metal hydroxides are alkaline substances that are caustic. These include sodium hydroxide, or caustic soda, and potassium hydroxide, or caustic potash. The corrosive action of caustic compounds is evoked by the figurative use of the word *caustic*, which refers to remarks or attitudes that are wounding.

21 charisma (kə-rĭz′mə)

noun

Exceptional personal magnetism or charm.

> On a clear morning in late September 1900, a lanky young man . . . stood among the more than 500 freshmen gathered to register at Harvard. Though neither a brilliant scholar nor a talented athlete, the young man had a certain **charisma** about him — a classmate later described him as "gray-eyed, cool, self-possessed, intelligent [with] the warmest, most friendly, and understanding smile." . . . His name was Franklin Delano Roosevelt, and in 1933 he became the fourth graduate of Harvard College to serve as president of the United States.
>
> — "It Wasn't So Easy for Roosevelt, Either,"
> *New York Times*, July 31, 2005

> Effective leadership doesn't depend on **charisma**. Dwight Eisenhower, George Marshall, and Harry Truman were singularly effective leaders, yet none possessed any more **charisma** than a dead mackerel. . . . Indeed, **charisma** becomes the undoing of leaders. It makes them inflexible, convinced of their own infallibility, unable to change. This is what happened to Stalin, Hitler, and Mao, and it is a commonplace in the study of ancient history that only Alexander the Great's early death saved him from becoming an ineffectual failure.
>
> — Peter F. Drucker, "Leadership as Work," in
> *The Essential Drucker: The Best of Sixty Years*
> *of Peter Drucker's Essential Writings on*
> *Management*, 2001

[From Greek *kharisma*, divine favor, from *kharizesthai*, to favor, from *kharis*, favor.]

cloying (kloi′ĭng)

adjective

Causing distaste or disgust because of an excess of something originally pleasant.

> Fifth Avenue was pink and white under pink and white clouds in a fluttering wind that was fresh after the **cloying** talk and choke of tobacco smoke and cocktails. She waved the taxi starter off merrily and smiled at him.
>
> — John Dos Passos, *Manhattan Transfer*, 1925

> The morning programs have always put an enormous premium on the "likability" of their on-air personalities, to an often **cloying** degree.
>
> — Ken Auletta, "The Dawn Patrol: The Curious Rise of Morning Television and the Future of Network News," *The New Yorker*, August 8, 2005

[Short for obsolete English *accloy,* to clog, from Middle English *acloien,* from Old French *encloer,* to drive a nail into, from Medieval Latin *inclāvāre* : *in-* in, into + *clāvāre,* to nail (from *clāvus,* nail).]

déjà vu (dā′-zhä vōō′)

noun

An impression of having seen or experienced something before.

> ROGER: Fox. Buddy D. Is this **déjà vu**? What's it been, a year, year and a half?
>
> BUD: I hear you're moving up in the world. Senior associate. Not bad . . . not bad. How's Margie?
>
> ROGER: Can't complain. Got a house in Oyster Bay, you know. Market treating you good?
>
> [. . .]
>
> BUD: The hours are hell, but the cash is starting to tumble in. I know this guy who has an ironclad way of making money. I can't lose and I can't get hurt.
>
> —from the film *Wall Street*, 1987

> Peter had also paid a visit to a Beverly Hills numerologist, he told a friend. "She said that in one incarnation I had been a priest in Roman days. You know — it's the old **déjà vu** thing, but every time I've been to Rome I've felt it — especially one night in the Circus Maximus. It's now a car park. About three in the morning I was sitting right there thinking about all the Christians who had been sacrificed to the lions and feeling that I must have been there."
>
> — Ed Sikov, *Mr. Strangelove: A Biography of Peter Sellers*, 2002

[From French *déjà vu* : *déjà*, already + *vu*, seen.]

dichotomy (dī-kŏt′ə-mē)

noun

A division into two contrasting things or parts.

> Being bohemian or counterculture, or alternative or whatever you want to call it — used to be all about **dichotomy**: you chose one life at the expense of another. Opt out of corporate life to run a literary magazine, and you had to live in a fifth-floor walkup, shop in thrift stores, drive an old VW bug and eat at hole-in-the-wall cafes. On the other hand, you got to cling to your unsullied ideals and aesthetic sense.
>
> — Rob Walker, "Fauxhemian Rhapsody," *New York Times*, January 23, 2000

> The distinction between mind and body is an artificial **dichotomy**, a discrimination which is unquestionably based far more on the peculiarity of intellectual understanding than on the nature of things.
>
> — Carl Jung, *Modern Man in Search of a Soul*, 1933

[From Greek *dikhotomiā,* from *dikhotomos,* divided in two : *dikho-,* in two (from *dikha*) + *temnein,* to cut.]

dilettante (dĭl′ĭ-tänt′)

noun

A person with a superficial interest in an art or field of knowledge; a dabbler.

adjective

Superficial; amateurish.

> Before long, I'd catalogued the various types who frequented the pool. There were the social butterflies. . . . They were wholly unimpressed with the fact that what they were in was a *swimming* not a standing pool. Then there were the **dilettantes**, who surface-dived like inept porpoises, essaying a few strokes now and then, sometimes with water weights strapped to their arms and legs. Often as not, they would swim the width of the pool rather than the length and, consequently, were almost impossible to avoid.
>
> — Katherine Merlin, "Swimming in a Little Pool Without Lanes: A Short Course in Survival," *Sports Illustrated*, May 14, 1984

> Her father's obsession with fleas, however, was not a **dilettante** enthusiasm, but a serious scientific interest. He had identified the flea that carries plague, *Xenopsylla cheopis Rothschild*, and had written more than 150 papers on the creatures.
>
> — "Miriam Rothschild," *The Economist*, February 5, 2005

[From Italian *dilettante*, lover of the arts, from present participle of *dilettare*, to delight, from Latin *dēlectāre* : *dē-*, intensive prefix + *lactāre*, to allure, wheedle, from *lacere*, to allure.]

---

disheveled *or* dishevelled (dĭ-shĕvʹəld)

adjective

Being in loose disarray; marked by disorder; untidy.

> ... and what would Roland do, and what would be done to Roland, if he were discovered like this, hiding, guilty-faced, with Babs Hendrick sprawled on the sofa, helpless in sleep, her hair **disheveled** and her clothing in disarray?
>
> — Joyce Carol Oates, "The High School Sweetheart," *Playboy*, January 2001

[From Middle English *discheveled*, from Old French *deschevele*, past participle of *descheveler*, to disarrange the hair : *des-*, apart (from Latin *dis-*) + *chevel*, hair (from Latin *capillus*).]

The meaning of *disheveled* suggests that the first part of the word is a prefix, *dis-*, meaning roughly "undo, do the opposite of." But what then is the rest of the word? Was there once a verb *hevel*? Not exactly.

Disheveled comes from Middle English *discheveled*, meaning specifically "having no hat or headdress on, and therefore (since a hat or headdress kept the hair in place) having one's hair in disorder." The Middle English word in turn comes from Old French *deschevele*, "having one's hair in disorder," which is in fact the past participle of the verb *descheveler*. This Old French verb was created by adding the prefix *des-*, "apart, away, with the opposite effect," to the noun *chevel*, "hair." (Readers who know Modern French will recognize *chevel* as the ancestor of Modern French *cheveu*, "hair.") *Descheveler* thus literally meant "to do apart the hair, undo one's hairdo." And so the *shevel* in *dishevel* simply comes from the Old French word for "hair." In modern English, of course, more than hair can be disheveled.

élan (ā-län′)

noun

1. Enthusiastic vigor and liveliness. **2.** Distinctive style or flair.

> The head shot of O'Fallon was inconclusive. Her eyes were too close together, Alma said, her chin was too broad, and her bobbed hair was not flattering to her features. Still, there was something effervescent about her, some spark of mischief or humor lurking in her gaze, a bright inner **élan**.
>
> —Paul Auster, *The Book of Illusions*, 2002

> With *Out of Sight*, Soderbergh found his niche. He now operates within Hollywood like a loyal opposition, making genre films with a grace and flair that eludes most directors employed by studios. He is not above a trivial caper movie like *Ocean's Eleven*, but invests it with such **élan** that it becomes pure pleasure to watch.
>
> —David Gritten, "Power Behind the Screen," http://www.telegraph.co.uk/arts, August 2, 2003

[From French *élan*, from Old French *eslan*, rush, from *eslancer*, to hurl : *es-*, out (from Latin *ex-*) + *lancer*, to throw (from Late Latin *lanceāre*, to throw a lance, from Latin *lancea*, lance).]

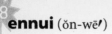

ennui (ŏn-wēʹ)

noun

Listlessness and dissatisfaction resulting from lack of interest; boredom.

> If we were always indeed getting our living, and regulating our lives according to the last and best mode we had learned, we should never be troubled with **ennui**. Follow your genius closely enough, and it will not fail to show you a fresh prospect every hour. . . . I kept neither dog, cat, cow, pig, nor hens, so that you would have said there was a deficiency of domestic sounds; neither the churn, nor the spinning wheel, nor even the singing of the kettle, nor the hissing of the urn, nor children crying, to comfort one. An old-fashioned man would have lost his senses or died of **ennui** before this.
>
> — Henry David Thoreau, *Walden*, 1854

[From French *ennui*, from Old French *enui*, from *ennuyer*, to annoy, bore, from Vulgar Latin **inodiāre*, to make odious, from Latin *in odiō*, odious : *in*, in + *odiō*, ablative form of *odium*, hatred.]

➤ The phrase *mihi in odiō est* (literally translated as "to me in a condition of dislike or hatred is"), meaning "I hate or dislike," gave rise to the Vulgar Latin verb **inodiāre*, "to make odious," the source of the Old French verb *ennuyer* or *anoier*, "to annoy, bore." This verb became the English word *anoien*, or *annoy*. A noun meaning "worry, boredom" was derived from *ennuyer* and became *ennui* in modern French. The noun *ennui* was borrowed into English in the 18th century.

epitome (ĭ-pĭt′ə-mē)

noun

The best or most representative example of a class or type.

> Mr. Amram, who lives on a farm in Putnam Valley, endures a schedule of concerts, lectures and jazz performances that might tire someone half his age, and he still finds time to compose. Viewed as the **epitome** of cool because of his early friendship with Jack Kerouac and the original circle of Beat poets, as well as for his unstuffy eclecticism, he is also known for his warmth and positivity.

> — Roberta Hershenson, "Not Going Softly, but Still Headlining and Swinging to the Beat," *New York Times*, November 13, 2005

> Indifference, to me, is the **epitome** of evil.

> — Elie Wiesel, "Humankind: Wisdom, Philosophy & Other Musings," *US News & World Report*, October 27, 1986

[From Latin *epitomē*, a summary, from Greek, an abridgment, from *epitemnein*, to cut short : *epi-*, upon, over, further + *temnein*, to cut.]

equanimity (ē′kwə-nĭm′ĭ-tē *or* ĕk′wə-nĭm′ĭ-tē)

noun

The quality of being calm and even-tempered; composure.

> CECILY: It is always painful to part from people whom one has known for a very brief space of time. The absence of old friends one can endure with **equanimity**. But even a momentary separation from anyone to whom one has just been introduced is almost unbearable.
>
> — Oscar Wilde, *The Importance of Being Earnest*, 1895

> Alfred Nobel, a half-century ago, foresaw with prophetic vision that if the complacent mankind of his day could, with **equanimity**, contemplate war, the day would soon inevitably come when man would be confronted with the fateful alternative of peace or reversion to the Dark Ages.
>
> — Ralph Bunche, Nobel Lecture, December 11, 1950

[From Latin *aequanimitās*, from *aequanimus*, even-tempered, impartial : *aequus*, even + *animus*, mind.]

equivocate (ĭ′kwĭv′ə-kāt′)

verb

To use vague or ambiguous language in order to avoid committing oneself to a position or to deceive someone.

> I am in earnest — I will not **equivocate** — I will not excuse — I will not retreat a single inch — and I will be heard!
>
> — William Lloyd Garrison, *The Liberator*,
> January 1, 1831

> Never in the history of the world did it dawn upon the human mind as it dawned upon your ancestors, what it would mean for men to be free. They got the vision of a government in which the people would be the supreme power. . . . They did not **equivocate** in a single word when they wrote the Declaration of Independence; no one can dream that these men had not got the sublimest ideal of democracy which had ever dawned upon the souls of men.
>
> — Anna Howard Shaw, "The Fundamental Principle of a Republic," speech given in Albany, New York, June 21, 1915

[From Middle English *equivocaten*, from Medieval Latin *aequivocāre, aequivocāt-*, from Late Latin *aequivocus*, equivocal : *aequus*, even, equal + *vocāre*, to call.]

esoteric (ĕs′ə-tĕr′ĭk)

adjective

Intended for or understood by only a restricted number of people.

> Without the controlling power of science, consumer demand for high-quality table wine never could have been satisfied, and fine wine would have had to remain an **esoteric** luxury enjoyed by only a privileged few.
>
> — Paul Lukacs, *American Vintage*, 2000

> The young modernists, Ezra Pound and T.S. Eliot, found Yeats's preoccupation with occultism silly, and Yeats knew that he must downplay his **esoteric** interests if the new, modernist literary establishment were to accept him.
>
> — Susan Johnston Graf, *W.B. Yeats: Twentieth-Century Magus*, 2000

[From Greek *esōterikos*, from *esōterō*, comparative of *esō*, within.]

euphemism (yōō′fə-mĭz′əm)

noun

1. A mild, indirect, or vague word used instead of one considered harsh, blunt, or offensive. **2.** The use of such words.

> Except in times of crisis, and sometimes even then, his schedule allowed him at least two or three hours for "personal staff time," a phrase that on the 1980 campaign plane had been considered a **euphemism** for "nap time." Meese laughed when I told him the campaign joke

that Reagan's best-known movie had been reissued under the title "Staff Time for Bonzo."

— Lou Cannon, *President Reagan: The Role of a
Lifetime*, 1991

Totalitarianism and other forms of tyranny flourish on
euphemism — calling mass killings or deportations
"ethnic cleansings" for instance; therefore seeing and
naming the object for what it really is can be a weapon
for political liberty.

— Thomas L. Jeffers, editor, *The Norman
Podhoretz Reader*, 2004

[From Greek *euphēmismos*, from *euphēmizein*, to use
auspicious words, from *euphēmiā*, use of auspicious words :
eu-, good + *phēmē* , speech.]

34

fait accompli (fā′tä-kôm-plē′ *or* fĕt′ä-kôm-plē′)

noun

An accomplished, presumably irreversible deed or fact.

It was eight weeks ago today...that information reached
us that the Argentine fleet was sailing toward the Falk-
lands. There were those who said we should have accepted the Argentine invasion as a **fait accompli**. But
whenever the rule of force as distinct from the rule of
law is seen to succeed, the world moves a step closer to
anarchy.

— Margaret Thatcher, speech to the Conservative
Women's Conference, May 26, 1982

[From French *fait accompli* : *fait*, fact + *accompli*, accomplished, past participle of *accomplir*, to accomplish, complete.]

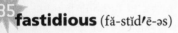

fastidious (fă-stĭd′ē-əs)

adjective

1. Possessing or displaying meticulous attention to detail. **2.** Excessively scrupulous or sensitive, especially in matters of taste.

> With a trusted Pygmy tracker, he would follow one group of gorillas discreetly but persistently for all of one day or several, holding back at distance enough (several hundred yards) to leave them unaware of his presence. Such **fastidious** tracking allowed him to learn what they had been eating, how many nests they had built, and how to make deductions about group size, ages, gender, while minimizing the chance that he'd spook these very shy primates.
>
> — David Quammen, "Megatransect,"
> *National Geographic*, 2000

[From Middle English *fastidious,* squeamish, particular, haughty, from Old French *fastidieux,* from Latin *fastīdiōsus,* from *fastīdium,* squeamishness, haughtiness, probably from *fastus,* disdain.]

GEORGE [*Furious with his father*]: I cannot believe you are seriously suggesting Miss Swartz as the companion of my heart and hearth!

MR. OSBORN: Why not?

GEORGE: Well, to begin with, she's not English.

MR. OSBORN: Hoity-toity! Less **fastidious**, if you please!

— from the film *Vanity Fair*, 2004

faux pas (fō pä′)

noun
Plural: **faux pas** (fō päz′)

A social blunder.

> PENNY MARSHALL: Here's Jane, a wild and beguiling gypsy ready to set your heart aflame if not for one fashion **faux pas**.
>
> ROB REINER: Jane is wearing a hamster head. Don't wear hamster heads; you've got a face — let's see it.
>
> — from the TV show *Saturday Night Live*, October 25, 1975

> When I had gone through all the magazines and even had read several of the articles, I began to fret that I might have committed a **faux pas** by coming in without making an appointment. But it was too late to worry about that, so I continued to wait.
>
> — Janet Langhart Cohen, *From Rage to Reason: My Life in Two Americas*, 2004

[From French *faux pas* : *faux,* false (from Old French *fals,* from Latin *falsus,* from past participle of *fallere,* to deceive) + *pas*, step (from Old French, from Latin *passus,* from past participle of *pandere,* to stretch, spread out).]

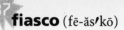

fiasco (fē-ăs′kō)

noun

A complete failure.

> ANNOUNCER: This reporter is stunned! The Charlestown Chiefs are not fighting back! . . . The Chiefs' performance tonight has got to be a bitter disappointment to these 4,000-odd Charlestown fans who have packed this War Memorial and paid good money to witness this — this **fiasco**.
>
> — from the film *Slap Shot*, 1977

> Jerome Robbins liked to say that you do your best work after your biggest disasters. For one thing, it's so painful it almost guarantees that you won't make those mistakes again. Also, you have nothing to lose; you've hit bottom, and the only place to go is up. A **fiasco** compels you to change dramatically.
>
> — Twyla Tharp, *The Creative Habit*, 2003

> The play dragged on, and seemed interminable. Half of the audience went out, tramping in heavy boots, and laughing. The whole thing was a **fiasco**. The last act was played to almost empty benches. The curtain went down on a titter, and some groans.
>
> — Oscar Wilde, *The Picture of Dorian Gray*, 1891

[From French *fiasco*, from Italian *fare fiasco*, to make a bottle, fail, from *fiasco*, bottle (perhaps translation of French *bouteille*, bottle, error, used by the French for linguistic errors committed by Italian actors on the 18th-century French stage), from Late Latin *flascō*, of Germanic origin.]

38 finagle (fə-nā'gəl)

verb

To obtain or achieve something by cleverness or deviousness, especially in using words.

> From there I'd driven across hundreds of miles of stupid desert in a disposable diaper of a Korean rental car and **finagled** a ride out of Dhahran on an airliner chartered by an English TV company to take its people and gear to the next place foreigners decide to get killed.
>
> — P.J. O'Rourke, *Give War a Chance,* 1992

> I told my mom I thought this Greatest Generation thing was getting a little out of hand.
> She gave me a steely look.
> "We saved your butt," she said.
> She began reminiscing about the way she **finagled** to get meat during the war by finding a vegetarian family in the neighborhood and trading her vegetable ration card for their meat ration card.
>
> — Maureen Dowd, "Liberties: The Gabbiest Generation," *New York Times,* April 25, 2001

[Probably from dialectal English *fainaigue,* to cheat.]

39 Freudian slip (froi'dē-ən)

noun

A verbal mistake that is thought to reveal an unconscious belief, thought, or emotion.

> A newspaper misreported the title of [Lise] Meitner's first lecture, "Problems of Cosmic Physics," as "Problems

of Cosmetic Physics"—either a **Freudian slip** or an intentional slight.

> —Gerhard Sonnert with Gerald Holton, *Who Succeeds in Science? The Gender Dimension*, 1995

"What do you want, you and Martin?"

I clutched my throat. "*Jeff*. You're supposed to be my friend. Don't marry me off to Martin."

"**Freudian slip**. You and Jeff," she said. I didn't know another soul who blushed.

I said, "Can you even imagine living with Martin? One minute everything's fine, the next minute you're in the volcano. I love the guy like I love my right arm, but I wouldn't want to live with him."

"I meant to say Jeff."

> —Erin McGraw, *The Good Life*, 2004

The term *Freudian slip* originates from the work of the Austrian neurologist Sigmund Freud (1856–1939), who first described the psychoanalytic theory of psychological development. According to Freud, the mind is divided into three levels of consciousness—the conscious, which represents awareness of everyday life; the unconscious, which contains elements that are not subject to conscious perception or control but can affect conscious thoughts and behavior; and the preconscious (popularly called the subconscious), which contains material that has been repressed to a certain extent but can be brought into conscious awareness with therapy.

In his 1901 book *The Psychopathology of Everyday Life* (*Zur Psychopathologie des Alltagslebens*), Freud referred to *Versprechen* (translated in 1914 as "slip of the tongue") and *Fehlleistung* ("faulty action"), a general error of thought, speech, or action resulting from wishes, conflicts, or other psychological material from the unconscious or preconscious mind that the speaker manifests unwittingly. This led to the contemporary term *Freudian slip*, a verbal mistake that shows a person's unconscious thoughts or wishes.

glib (glĭb)

adjective

1. Performed with a natural, offhand ease. **2.** Marked by ease and fluency of speech or writing that suggests or stems from insincerity, superficiality, or deceitfulness.

> She sat and talked about the dinner on the train, which had been so poor; about London, about dances. She was really very nervous, and chattered from fear. Morel sat all the time smoking his thick twist tobacco, watching her, and listening to her **glib** London speech, as he puffed.
>
> — D.H. Lawrence, *Sons and Lovers*, 1913

> Hare's play never ignites. He drizzles **glib** dialogue over their encounter; like coulis on a plate, it makes the dish look more appetizing than it actually is.
>
> — John Lahr, "Dames at Sea: Mouth-to-Mouth Resuscitation in David Hare's New Play," *The New Yorker*, October 28, 2002

[Possibly shortening of *glibbery*, slippery, possibly from Low German *glibberig*, smooth, slippery, from Middle Low German *glibberich* : *glibber*, jelly (akin to dialectal Dutch *glib*, curds) + *-ich*, adjectival suffix.]

gregarious (grĭ-gâr′ē-əs)

adjective

Seeking and enjoying the company of others; sociable.

> Biologically speaking, man is a moderately **gregarious**, not a completely social animal — a creature more like a wolf, let us say, or an elephant, than like a bee or an ant.
>
> — Aldous Huxley, *Brave New World Revisited*, 1959

> He saw himself as a voice crying in the wilderness, because Mary was a **gregarious** queen who enjoyed the constant cycle of banquets, dancing, masques and dramatic entertainments she had become used to in France.
>
> — John Guy, *Queen of Scots: The True Life of Mary Stuart*, 2004

[From Latin *gregārius*, belonging to a flock, from *grex, greg-*, flock.]

harbinger (här′bĭn-jər)

noun

Something that indicates or foreshadows what is to come; a forerunner.

> Today, by midafternoon massive storm clouds and black horizons of rain have formed. Two scarlet macaws are dollops of red in the green canopy; against the dark western sky, they seem radiant. At dusk, lightning rends the turning clouds, a **harbinger** of the rainy season. Downdrafts, cold and heavy with moisture, tousle the river surface and the treetops.
>
> — David Campbell, *A Land of Ghosts*, 2005

> Despite their beauty, comets have cast a sinister shadow over human history, myth and folklore. Across centuries and civilizations, comets were often viewed as **harbingers** of doom, their unpredictable arrival in the night sky seen as foreshadowing wars, plagues and natural disasters.
>
> — Jeffrey Kaye, from the TV show *The NewsHour with Jim Lehrer*, June 29, 2005

[From Middle English *herbengar,* person sent ahead to arrange lodgings, from Old French *herbergeor,* from *herbergier,* to provide lodging for, from *herberge,* lodging, of Germanic origin (akin to Old High German *heriberga,* army shelter, lodging : *heri,* army + *berga,* shelter).]

43 hedonist (hĕd′n-ĭst)

noun

A person who is devoted to the pursuit of pleasure, especially to the pleasures of the senses.

> Here is where designer homespun leads us all. Today's **hedonists** revolt against the work ethic while dressed in the garb of the hardest around-the-clock workers: farmers, ranchhands, fishermen, lumberjacks, bakers. Could there be anything more ironic?
>
> — Melvin Maddocks, "Low Chic and the Sweatshirt," *Christian Science Monitor*, June 5, 1980

> "We aren't here for a party," Agamemnon said. Xerxes, though, had always seemed disappointed that he could no longer indulge in fine foods; he had been a **hedonist** in his human days. Now he just gave a mechanical sigh and admired his surroundings.
>
> — Brian Herbert and Kevin J. Anderson, *Dune: The Machine Crusade*, 2003

[From Greek *hēdonē*, pleasure.]

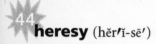

heresy (hĕr′ĭ-sē′)

noun

1. An opinion or a teaching at variance with established beliefs or opinions. **2.** Adherence to such an
opinion or teaching.

> He was not about to compromise a promising career by
> promulgating a **heresy** that he could not prove. What
> then was his **heresy**? A belief in evolution itself.
>
> — Stephen Jay Gould, *Ever Since Darwin:*
> *Relations in Natural History*, 1977

> That the European Union barreled ahead was not surpris-
> ing, given that questioning the timetable for the single
> currency, much less the goal, is considered **heresy** out-
> side of Britain and Denmark, the two European Union
> members that have demanded the right not to take part.
>
> — Richard W. Stevenson, "A European Currency:
> French Strikes Pose Harsh Test," *New York*
> *Times*, December 17, 1995

[From Middle English *heresie,* from Old French, from Late
Latin *haeresis,* from Late Greek *hairesis,* from Greek, a
choosing, faction, from *haireisthai,* to choose.]

The same was self-evidently true of Pauline Gore. . . . Gore, a lawyer by training at a time when female lawyers were rare, and a truly bright woman who had an enormous impact on the careers of both her husband and her son, was also a faithful, publicly uncomplaining attendee at the time-devouring, mind-numbing social ceremonies of wifedom. Such women were just a few of the many who, though they might quietly confide their own impatience with these ceremonies, were at pains to give no offense and commit no **heresy**—starting with the major **heresy** of not turning up—that would call unfavorable attention to themselves and by extension do some damage to their husbands' standing in the political/governmental community.

—Meg Greenfield,
Washington, 2001

idiosyncratic (ĭd′ē-ō-sĭng-krăt′ĭk)

adjective

Peculiar to a specific individual or group.

> In the Namib Desert, one of the oldest on earth, there is a dazzling array of creatures with **idiosyncratic** adaptations to the extreme heat and dryness: a lizard that hops from foot to foot to diffuse heat absorption; a beetle that curls into a ball to roll down dunes to conserve energy; a spider that spins a small cone-shaped web to track and condense dew; and a fog collector beetle.
>
> — Marq de Villiers, *Water: The Fate of Our Most Precious Resource*, 1999

> Even in his toughest gangster roles, Bogart was sympathetic. Always the enemy of emotion, he nonchalantly accepted his inevitable doom while conveying an **idiosyncratic** mixture of high tension and sexy charm.
>
> — Jeffrey Meyers, *Bogart: A Life in Hollywood*, 1997

[From Greek *idiosunkrāsiā* : *idios,* personal, private + *sunkrāsis,* mixture, temperament (from *sun-,* together, with + *krāsis,* a mixing).]

---

idyllic (ī-dĭl′ĭk)

adjective

Tranquil, carefree, or picturesque.

> On this occasion he had fallen at once into a dreamless sleep. One arm dropped over the edge of the bed, one leg was arched, and the unfinished part of his laugh was stranded on his mouth, which was open, showing the little pearls. Thus defenceless Hook found him. He stood silent at the foot of the tree looking across the chamber at his enemy. Did no feeling of compassion stir his sombre breast? The man was not wholly evil; . . . and, let it be frankly admitted, the **idyllic** nature of the scene stirred him profoundly.
>
> — J.M. Barrie, *Peter Pan*, 1904

> Rigorously trained physicians knew enough to make a difference. Even when ignorant about the medical condition, which was often, a doctor was at the patient's home, keeping vigil at the bedside. Hospitalization was the exception. The doctor knew the patient as a person, was familiar with the family, and had a sound notion of the prevailing psychological and social stresses. In present-day America, this **idyllic** scene has vanished. In the large urban sprawl where most of the population resides, a doctor confronts a stranger.
>
> — Bernard Lown, *The Lost Art of Healing*, 1996

[From *idyll*, short poem on a pastoral theme, narrative poem on a romantic theme, from Latin *īdyllium*, pastoral poem, from Greek *eidullion*, diminutive of *eidos*, form, figure.]

indelicate (ĭn-dĕl′ĭ-kĭt)

adjective

Marked by a lack of good taste or consideration for the feelings of others; tactless or improper.

> The effect of taboo can be very powerful. Several generations ago, the simple anatomical terms *leg* and *breast* came to be regarded as highly **indelicate** in American speech. The unacceptability of these words required euphemisms not only for talking about the human body but even for talking about roast chicken and Thanksgiving turkeys, with the result that Americans began to speak of *dark meat* and *white meat*, as they still do today, even though *leg* and *breast* have more recently lost their **indelicate** status.
>
> — R.L. Trask, *Historical Linguistics*, 1996

> [Mr. Casaubon:] "My aunt made an unfortunate marriage. I never saw her."
>   Dorothea wondered a little, but felt that it would be **indelicate** just then to ask for any information which Mr. Casaubon did not proffer, and she turned to the window to admire the view.
>
> — George Eliot, *Middlemarch*, 1871

[From *in-*, not + Modern English *delicate*, from Middle English *delicat* and French *délicat* (both from Latin *dēlictus*, pleasing, akin to *dēlicia*, pleasure : *dē-*, intensive prefix + *lactāre*, to allure, wheedle, from *lacere*, to allure).]

infinitesimal (ĭn′fĭn-ĭ-tĕs′ə-məl)

adjective

Immeasurably or incalculably small.

> We cannot consider the question of our foreign policy without at the same time treating of the Army and the Navy. We now have a very small army indeed, one well-nigh **infinitesimal** when compared with the army of any other large nation. Of course the army we do have should be as nearly perfect of its kind and for its size as is possible.

> — President Theodore Roosevelt, State of the Union Address, December 5, 1905

> When George Bernard Shaw wrote *Saint Joan*, he had the immense advantage of having never known her. He had never seen her walk, never heard her talk, could never have been haunted by any of those **infinitesimal**, inimitable tones, turns, tics, quirks, which are different in every human being, and which make love and death such inexorably private affairs.

> — James Baldwin, *Price of the Ticket*, 1985

[From New Latin *īnfīnītēsimus*, infinite in rank, from Latin *īnfīnītus*, infinite : *in-*, not + *fīnītus*, finite, from past participle of *fīnīre*, to limit, from *fīnis*, end.]

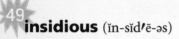

insidious (ĭn-sĭd′ē-əs)

adjective

Doing harm in a subtle or imperceptible manner;
treacherous.

> Against the **insidious** wiles of foreign influence (I con-
> jure you to believe me, fellow-citizens), the jealousy of a
> free people ought to be constantly awake; since history
> and experience prove, that foreign influence is one of
> the most baneful foes of Republican Government.
>
> — President George Washington, Farewell
> Address, September 17, 1796

[From Latin *īnsidiōsus*, from *īnsidiae*, ambush, from *īnsidēre*,
to sit upon, lie in wait for : *in-*, in, on + *sedēre*, to sit.]

MRS. TEASDALE: My purse has been stolen — the plans of war are in it.

GROUCHO [*Shouting*]: WHAT? [*Walks up and down puffing furiously on his cigar*]

MRS. TEASDALE: I . . . I may be wrong, but I suspect the Secretary of War.

GROUCHO [*Still pacing wildly*]: Don't bother me; I'm thinking. *What* was that?

MRS. TEASDALE: I said — I suspect the Secretary of War.

GROUCHO [*Stopping dead in his tracks*]: THIS IS TREASON! [*Strikes a pose, raising his clenched hands; then to Mrs. Teasdale scornfully*] What a fool I was to listen to your siren song and fall a helpless victim under the **insidious** spell of your irresistible charms.

MRS. TEASDALE: But —

GROUCHO [*Paying no attention*]: You satisfied your selfish whims, while nations tottered, dynasties rocked and the world plunged headlong into a chasm of chaos and oblivion — [*Throws her an arch look*] Not bad, eh?

— Harry Ruby, Bert Kalmar, and Grover Jones, *Cracked Ice*, a preliminary screenplay for the film *Duck Soup*, 1933

junket (jŭng′kĭt)

noun

A trip or tour, especially one taken by an official at public expense or by a person who is the guest of a business or agency seeking patronage.

> If your local critics or TV reporters are kind to this film, you might bear in mind that 78 of them were invited on a publicity **junket** to Jamaica, as part of the film's budget.
>
> — Pauline Kael, quoted in "Perils of Pauline," *Newsweek*, May 30, 1966

> I come to a naval complex of moors and piers, fringed by palms warped by millennia of offshore winds. Elsewhere commercial launches leave hourly for tours of the harbor, but I am booked on a military VIP **junket**. Judging by my fellow passengers, almost anyone can be a VIP.
>
> — William Manchester, *Goodbye, Darkness*, 1979

[From Middle English *jonket*, rush basket, a kind of food served on rushes, feast, from Old North French *jonquette*, rush basket, or Medieval Latin *iuncāta*, rush basket, both from Latin *iuncus*, rush.]

In English, a *junket* was originally a basket made of rushes. Beginning in the 1400s, the word also began to be used of a kind of dessert made from flavored milk and rennet that was prepared in a rush basket or served on a rush mat. *Junket* later came to refer to a variety of other sweet delicacies or fine foods. In the 1500s, the word acquired the meaning "banquet," and later, mostly in American English, the word also came to denote a festive outing or picnic. By the end of the 1800s, *junket* had begun to acquire its modern meaning and refer to a very specific kind of outing—a trip taken by a public official and disguised as official business or paid for by lobbyists.

kitsch (kĭch)

noun

Art or other objects appealing to popular taste, as by being gaudy or overly sentimental.

"Your mother walks in the door with three hundred sixty days' worth of Christmas mania, she's been obsessing since the previous January, and then, of course, *Where's that Austrian reindeer figurine — don't you like it? Don't you use it? Where is it? Where is it? Where is the Austrian reindeer figurine?* She's got her food obsessions, her money obsessions, her clothes obsessions, she's got the whole ten-piece set of baggage which my husband *used* to agree is *kind of a problem*, but now suddenly, out of the blue, he's taking *her* side. We're going to turn the house inside out looking for a piece of thirteen-dollar gift-store **kitsch** because it has sentimental value to your mother —"

— Jonathan Franzen, *The Corrections*, 2001

NAOMI: The dining room is where we dine. The bedroom is where we go to bed. The bathroom is where we take a bath. The kitchen is where we . . . cook. That doesn't sound right. The kitchen is where we . . . collect **kitsch**. Hummel figurines, Statue of Liberty salt and pepper shakers, underpants that say Home of the Whopper, and so on. **Kitsch**. The kitchen is where we look at **kitsch**.

— Christopher Durang, *Naomi in the Living Room*, from *Naomi in the Living Room and Other Short Plays*, 1998

[From German *Kitsch*, perhaps akin to *kitschen*, to scrape up street mud, smooth down (from a notion likening bad painting to mud scraped off streets or the skills of a bad painter to those of a street cleaner).]

litany (lĭt'n-ē)

noun

A repetitive recital or list.

> The working conditions in these meatpacking plants were brutal. In *The Jungle* (1906) Upton Sinclair described a **litany** of horrors: severe back and shoulder injuries, lacerations, amputations, exposure to dangerous chemicals, and memorably, a workplace accident in which a man fell into a vat and got turned into lard.
>
> — Eric Schlosser, *Fast Food Nation: The Dark Side of the All-American Meal*, 2001

[From Middle English *letanie,* prayer in the form of a litany, from Old French *letanie,* from Late Latin *litanīa,* from Late Greek *litaneia,* from Greek, entreaty, from *litaneuein,* to entreat, from *litanos,* entreating, from *litē,* supplication.]

Originally, the word *litany* designated a specific type of liturgical prayer. As part of the recitation of a litany, a member of the clergy or other leader pronounces a long series of varying supplications or invocations after which the congregation responds with a fixed formula, such as *Pray for us.* Alternating in this way between leader and congregation, litanies can be quite long, and the term *litany* therefore has come to refer to any tediously repetitive list.

Khrushchev repeated his by now familiar **litany** of threats: He would sign a peace treaty [with the German Democratic Republic] no matter what; Western access to Berlin would be cut off; if the West used force, a war was bound to be thermonuclear; though the United States and USSR might survive, America's European allies would be completely destroyed.

— William Taubman,
*Khrushchev: The Man
and His Era*, 2003

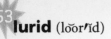

lurid (loŏr′ĭd)

adjective

Characterized by vivid description or explicit details that are meant to provoke or shock.

> The solution which Canada almost immediately found for such eruptions of violence in its North-West Territories was better than any the Americans had found in all the generations of their frontier history. When the exaggerated and **lurid** story of the Cypress Hills fight, getting dirtier as it went, like a summer whirlwind, reached Ottawa, it stirred up a fury of public feeling against Americans at large and against whiskey traders in particular.
>
> — Wallace Stegner, *Wolf Willow: A History, a Story, and a Memory of the Last Plains*, 1962

[From Latin *lūridus*, pale, from *lūror*, paleness.]

The English adjective *lurid* comes from Latin *lūridus*, "sickly yellow, sallow, wan," which could be used to describe the color of teeth or skin, for example. As an extension of the original meaning "sallow, wan," *lūridus* could even be used of things that are simply horrifying or ghastly, such as poisonous herbs or even the concept of death itself—the very thought of which makes a person grow pale. The Roman writer Pliny the Younger also used the Latin adjective to describe the unsettling color of the sun shining through a cloud of ash in his account of the devastating volcanic eruption that buried the city of Pompeii.

When *lurid* first appeared in English in the mid-1600s, the word described things that are pale in a sickly or disturbing way. *Lurid* could also be used of grayish, overcast skies. Later, in the 1700s, writers began to use *lurid* to describe the red glow of fire blazing dimly within smoke. In the 1800s, *lurid* came to mean "sensationalistic," its most common meaning today.

MARION: Sam. This is the last time.

SAM: For what?

MARION: For this. Meeting you in secret so we can be . . . secretive. You come down here on business trips and we steal lunch hours and . . . I wish you wouldn't even come.

SAM: All right. What do we do instead, write each other **lurid** love letters?

MARION [*Getting up from the bed*]: I have to go, Sam.

— from the film *Psycho,* 1960

Machiavellian (măk′ē-ə-věl′ē-ən)

adjective

Characterized by cunning and deceit.

> Had there been a clear successor available, Roosevelt would have found it very difficult to command support for a third term. The **Machiavellian** theory is therefore that he had carefully built up a number of competing possible successors, all of whom merely had to be exposed to the light of day for it to be obvious how inadequate they were. But this is always a risky course: very few politicians look worthy of the top jobs until they actually come to occupy them.
>
> — Roy Jenkins, *Franklin Delano Roosevelt*, 2003

> The business of the university is political, then, not simply because it is a place of **Machiavellian** intrigue, self-serving negotiation, passive aggression, devious alliance, and mind-numbing committee discussions — of which it is — but because it is a place where citizens critique knowledge in the service of defining happiness and a democratic community.
>
> — Eric Gould, *The University in a Corporate Culture*, 2003

[After Niccolò Machiavelli (1469–1527), Italian political theorist.]

Niccolò Machiavelli's two major works, *The Prince* and *Discourses on Livy*, describe the ways in which a determined ruler can achieve and maintain power through indifference to moral considerations. Machiavelli's political doctrine denies the relevance of morality in political affairs and holds that craft and deceit are justified in pursuing and maintaining political power. His works are characterized by an unflinchingly realistic evaluation of human relations, as in the following passage from *The Prince*:

> *Therefore it is to be noted that, when seizing a state, the invader should consider carefully all those injuries that are necessary for him to do; and to do them all at a single stroke, so that he does not have to repeat them every day, and to be able, by not repeating the injuries, to reassure the men of the state and to win them over by doing good to them. . . . For injuries should be done all at the same time, so that, since they are tasted less, they offend less.*

Machiavelli's theories are based on his experience as an administrator and diplomat in Florence during a tumultuous epoch in that city's history; he had ample opportunity to observe how crafty rulers could attain their goals and also how naïve or inattentive rulers could lose everything through carelessness. His soberly realistic assessments of human affairs led to the use of the word *Machiavellian* to describe any behavior or policy characterized by expediency, deceit, and cunning.

malaise (mă-lāz′)

noun

A general sense of unease.

> After the ninth round, Hoffman and Cantwell told Baer, who now seemed typically detached from the proceedings, exactly where he stood. "You're losing," Hoffman said as he doused Baer with a sponge. "Now go out there and end this."
>
> "No problem," Baer replied, muttering through his mouthpiece. He finally snapped out of his **malaise** and fought the tenth round as if it were the first.
>
> — Jeremy Schaap, *Cinderella Man: James Braddock, Max Baer, and the Greatest Upset in Boxing History*, 2005

> These travelers carried with them the infection of their own **malaise**, and their prose reduced even the landscape to melancholia and self-contempt.
>
> — Derek Walcott, Nobel Lecture, December 7, 1992

[From French *malaise*, from Old French : *mal-*, bad (from Latin, from *male*, badly, and *malus*, bad) + *aise*, elbowroom, physical comfort, ease, of obscure origin.]

malinger (mă-lĭng′gər)

verb

To fake illness in order to avoid work or duty.

> She was an Irish relative of Grandmother's, who had spent perhaps fifty years in China and was stopping off with us on her way to her death, a few months after she left us. . . . I was about eight then, I think, and already adept at **malingering**, just enough to stay home from school but still feel well enough to spend the whole day roaming in the hills with Cousin Lizzie.
>
> —M.F.K. Fisher, *Among Friends*, 1970

> In Cuba most cane was still cut by hand. Blackened from head to toe, their eyes smarting from the acrid dust, the men worked their way through the burned-over fields with their machetes in daytime temperatures that might exceed one hundred degrees Fahrenheit. They continued to complain. And to **malinger**.
>
> —Robert E. Quirk, *Fidel Castro*, 1993

[From French *malingre*, sickly, from Old French : perhaps *mal*, bad (from Latin *malus*) + *heingre, haingre*, emaciated (of obscure origin).]

57 **mantra** (măn′trə)

noun

A word or phrase that is expressed repeatedly, as in reaffirming an idea or motivating someone.

> The swamp is my friend, Braddock insisted to himself. Holding his M-16 above his head, wading through the cold chest-high water, pulling his combat boots out of muck, he repeated the **mantra** his survival instructors had drilled into him long ago when he'd joined the Rangers. The swamp is my friend.
>
> —David Morrell, *The Protector*, 2003

[From Sanskrit *mantraḥ*, sacred verbal formula.]

In Hinduism and Buddhism, a *mantra* is a sacred verbal formula recited, often repeatedly, as part of prayer, meditation, or incantation. A mantra can be an invocation of a god, a magic spell, a portion of scripture, or even a single syllable, like *Om*, that is believed to have mystical properties. Those who recite mantras believe that the power of the mantra can transcend the meaning of the phrase; the very sound of the words themselves creates favorable effects for those who recite them.

The English word *mantra* comes from Sanskrit, the sacred language of ancient India. The basic meaning of the Sanskrit word is "an instrument to think with"—that is, a means of contemplation—and *mantra* is related by common ancestry to English words like *mind, mental, mention,* and *reminiscent.*

maudlin (môd′lĭn)

adjective

Excessively sentimental.

> "You and I know, Ben, that Hugh has a heart, but we also know that he's not likely to lose it. Now don't look so grave. I don't mean anything bad by that. Lots of people never lose their hearts. They're simply made that way. Hugh's father's like that. . . . I can always say that if he hasn't lost his heart to someone as good as I am, he probably won't lose it to others. But we live in a **maudlin** world, where oodles of silly souls think that losing their heart is the great business of life. Whereas finding it might be the trick for most of them."
>
> — Louis Auchincloss, "The Atonement," from
> *The Atonement and Other Stories*, 1997

> I'm on a leash, everything so depressingly familiar. I'm tempted to write out all my recollections of our weekends, our evenings together, just so I can linger on them a bit more, but that would be **maudlin**, and you wouldn't like that — which is, of course, why I love you.
>
> — Adam Haslett, "Devotion," *The Yale Review*,
> Vol. 90, No. 3; 2002

[Alteration of *(Mary) Magdalene*, who was frequently depicted as a tearful penitent.]

mercenary (mûr′sə-nĕr′ē)

adjective

Motivated solely by a desire for monetary or material gain.

> **LADY BRACKNELL:** Never speak disrespectfully of Society, Algernon. Only people who can't get into it do that. [*To Cecily*] Dear child, of course you know that Algernon has nothing but his debts to depend upon. But I do not approve of **mercenary** marriages. When I married Lord Bracknell I had no fortune of any kind. But I never dreamed for a moment of allowing that to stand in my way.
>
> — Oscar Wilde, *The Importance of Being Earnest*, 1895

> And finally, parents emigrating west in search of greater opportunity quite often left behind even very young children who had good jobs. Such parents were not necessarily heartless or **mercenary**; generally they saw themselves as sparing the child from the serious risks and hardship of frontier life.
>
> — Stephen O'Connor, *Orphan Trains*, 2001

[From Middle English *mercenarie,* a hireling, from Old French *mercenaire,* mercenary, a hireling, from Latin *mercēnnārius,* from mercēs, wages, price.]

> The word *mercenary* can also be used as a noun to refer to a hireling or a person who works merely for personal gain. In particular, *mercenary* is frequently used to designate a professional soldier hired for service in a foreign army.

minimalist (mĭn′ə-mə-lĭst)

adjective

Characterized by the use of only the simplest or most essential elements, as in the arts, literature, or design.

ANN: I just wanted to come by and see what the apartment looked like, you know, with furniture.

GRAHAM [*In the other room, dressing*]: Yeah, you know, I'm afraid there's not much to see. I'm sort of cultivating this **minimalist** vibe.

ANN: You could use a bookshelf.

GRAHAM [*Distracted, buttoning his shirt*]: Yeah . . . yeah, you think so? I [*Laughs*], you know, they're all library books.

— from the film *Sex, Lies, and Videotape*, 1989

What an irony that we, who have always depended on this scientific excellence and industrial might to protect us, are threatened not by a First World or even Second or Third World country, but by a terrorist guerrilla group, rootless in terms of nationhood and with a medieval vision for the future. Yet this group has managed to find exceptional financing and to adapt itself to a shrewd if **minimalist** application of borrowed or stolen modern technology.

— David Halberstam, "Who We Are," *Vanity Fair*, November 2001

[From *minimum,* from the neuter form of Latin *minimus,* least.]

misnomer (mĭs-nō′mər)

noun

A name wrongly or unsuitably applied to a person or an object.

> To the public, the model means that the universe began from a single point, underwent an explosion, and has been flying apart ever since. However, the big bang is not an explosion at all. This is an unfortunate **misnomer** that cosmologists would like to correct. But the bad name has stuck. The big bang is the expansion or stretching of space. It is not that things are flying out from a point. Rather, all things are moving away from each other.
>
> — Paul J. Steinhardt, "A Brief Introduction to the Ekpyrotic Universe," http://wwwphysics.princeton.edu/~steinh/npr/, 2004

> Finding oneself was a **misnomer**: a self is not found but made; and the anti-hero, anti-history bias was an obstacle to making it, because a starting point from the past was missing; it had to be made from scratch.
>
> — Jacques Barzun, *From Dawn to Decadence*, 2000

[From Middle English *misnoumer*, from Old French *mesnomer*, to misname : *mes-*, wrongly + *nommer*, to name (from Latin *nōmināre*, from *nōmen*, name).]

narcissist (när′sĭ-sĭst)

noun

One who is excessively preoccupied with oneself; an extremely self-centered person.

> Of course, for a **narcissist**, privacy is a relative concept. Often, it's just part of the performance. *Private*, when the celebrity uses the word, means many things, perhaps "I'm classy" or "I don't go to nightclubs" or "I'm shy," but what it rarely means is "I'm private" and certainly not when a semi-naked photo shoot is involved.
>
> — Vanessa Grigoriadis, "Celebrity and Its Discontents: A Diagnosis," *New York Magazine*, July 2005

> STEIN: No . . . I have never truly felt a liking or a loving for anyone on this planet. Anyone excluding myself . . . and Italy, of course.
>
> ALICE: That does seem odd, doesn't it?
>
> STEIN: Well, to a supreme **narcissist** it is a way of life.
>
> ALICE [*Laughing*]: And that is how you picture yourself? As a supreme **narcissist**?
>
> STEIN: To a certain extent, yes. I have never truly loved anyone else. Perhaps that is why I "settled" into writing. They say to write best, you should write what you know. I have never known anything other than myself.
>
> — Charles L. Cron, *The Expatriates*, 1994

[After *Narcissus*, a figure of classical mythology, from Greek *narkissos*, the narcissus flower.]

As the Roman poet Ovid tells the story in his work *Metamorphoses*, Narcissus was a beautiful young man, the son of a nymph and a river-god. He had many admirers but spurned them all, including the nymph Echo. One of Narcissus's many rejected lovers cursed him for his hardheartedness. "Let him love too, and be unable to obtain the one he loves!" And so it happened.

While hunting, Narcissus came to a pool of water shaded by a little wood. He leaned down to drink and saw the image of a charming youth reflected in the water. Instantly he fell in love with the handsome face, and he remained rooted to the banks of the pool, contemplating his own image. Narcissus tried to kiss the object of his desire, but it always eluded his embrace. He addressed loving words to the face he saw. Echo, who had been condemned by Hera, the queen of the gods, to repeat the speech of others, heard him and took pity on him. Echo repeated his words so that Narcissus thought his lover was answering him.

Eventually Narcissus pined away and died of his unfulfilled love. When the nymphs came to give him a proper funeral, they found the narcissus flower nodding over the pool in place of his body.

63 nirvana (nîr-vä′nə)

noun

An ideal condition of harmony, stability, or joy.

> A few minutes later, the desserts arrive — a chocolate torte with a dollop of mascarpone and zabaione cream; apple sorbet; strawberry bavaroise. All are exquisite, especially when paired with a local Malvasia wine, which is sweet, smooth and the colour of maple syrup. "Delicious," purrs Vittorio.
>
> Wilde was right about the power of a good dinner to make one forgive anything. As we slide into post-prandial **nirvana**, that glorious state when the appetite is calmed and all is right in the world, Vittorio's McDonald's confession already seems like a distant memory.
>
> —Carl Honoré, *In Praise of Slowness: How a Worldwide Movement Is Challenging the Cult of Speed*, 2004

[From Sanskrit *nirvāṇam*, blowing out, extinction, nirvana : *nis-, nir-*, out, away + *vāti*, it blows.]

For Buddhists, Hindus, and Jains, the Sanskrit term *nirvāṇam* denotes a fundamental concept — the ultimate goal of all religious practice in their respective religions — which is originally rather different from the idea of paradise in Christianity or Islam. In Buddhism, for instance, *nirvāṇam* denotes the ineffable condition of those who attain the highest wisdom and freedom from attachment, while in Hinduism the term describes the release from ignorance and from attachment usually achieved by mystical union with the supreme deity. In these Eastern schools of thought, worldly desires and the inevitable suffering that they cause are likened to the burning of fire. The goal of religious practice is to extinguish this fire by extinguishing the self — which will be blown out like a candle flame. Sanskrit *nirvāṇam* literally means "the act of blowing out, extinction (as of a flame)."

---

non sequitur (nŏn sĕk′wĭ-tər)

noun

A statement that does not follow logically from what precedes it.

> Anticipation began to plague her with such ferocity that the thought of a husband, on which all her hopes were pinned, threatened at times to send her into another attack. Amid tins of talc and boxes of bobby pins she would curl up on the floor of the storage room, speaking in **non sequiturs**. "I will never dip my feet in milk," she whimpered. "My face will never be painted with sandalwood paste. Who will rub me with turmeric? My name will never be printed with scarlet ink on a card."
>
> — Jhumpa Lahiri, *Interpreter of Maladies*, 1999

> On being told he was a grandfather, my father's answer was "Federico Fellini just died." This became an instant family joke, along with his other memorable **non sequiturs**. (If indeed it was a **non sequitur**. The translation might be "What do I care about your new baby when death is staring me in the face?")
>
> — Philip Lopate, "The Story of My Father," *Getting Personal*, 2003

[From Latin *nōn sequitur*, it does not follow : *nōn*, not + *sequitur*, third person singular present tense of *sequī*, to follow.]

nouveau riche (nōō'vō rēsh')

adjective

Characterized by newly acquired wealth, especially when it is flaunted.

From the novels of Henry James to Orson Welles's *Citizen Kane*, middle-class Americans have mocked the pathos of being **nouveau riche** — not knowing which fork to use at the banquet. Ralph Lauren, who comes from a past as humble as mine, has become very rich indeed, convincing middle-class Americans that if we buy a blue shirt with a polo player stitched on, we will look as gloriously bored and as golden as the old rich of Long Island.

> — Richard Rodriguez, from the TV show
> *The NewsHour with Jim Lehrer*,
> September 24, 2002

The good wood furniture, decorative silver plates, paintings of significant persons and picturesque landscapes, and historical and family artifacts that fill Doña Elena's apartment are arranged not as a flashy show of **nouveau riche** wealth designed to impress the visitor, but as a low-key expression of the good taste that comes with dignified social belonging.

> — Steve J. Stern, *Remembering Pinochet's Chile:*
> *On the Eve of London 1998*, 2004

[From French *nouveau riche* : *nouveau*, new + *riche*, rich.]

oblivion (ə-blĭv′ē-ən)

noun

1. The condition of being completely forgotten. **2.** A condition of total forgetfulness.

> The task force became a caricature of all bad committees: slow, political, aggravating. Most of the work was done by a small and dedicated subgroup. But other committee members and key line managers developed little interest in or understanding of this group's efforts, and next to none of the recommendations was implemented. The task force limped along for eighteen months and then faded into **oblivion**.
>
> — John P. Kotter, *Leading Change*, 1996

> I have a dim half-remembrance of long, anxious times of waiting and fearing; darkness in which there was not even the pain of hope to make present distress more poignant: and then long spells of **oblivion**, and the rising back to life as a diver coming up through a great press of water.
>
> — Bram Stoker, *Dracula*, 1897

[From Middle English *oblivioun*, from Old French *oblivion*, from Latin *oblīviō, oblīviōn-*, from *oblīvīscī*, to forget.]

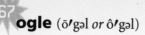

ogle (ō′gəl *or* ô′gəl)

verb

To stare at something, especially in a desirous or impertinent manner.

> There was an opera house with Greek pillars and a fountain in which children tossed pennies. She couldn't resist peering into every shop window to **ogle** the things that weren't available in Minerva.
>
> — Mary Sharratt, *The Real Minerva*, 2004

> In particular, he saw her outlined against the deep green waters, in which squadrons of silvery fish wheeled incessantly, or **ogled** her for a moment, pressing their distorted mouths against the glass, quivering their tails straight out behind them.
>
> — Virginia Woolf, *Night and Day*, 1919

> They came into town once a week, their skin scummy and stinking and blackened from oil and caked-on dirt, to get a bath and a shave at the barbershop. Young children **ogled** at them when they appeared because it was unimaginable, even by the standards of children, to find anyone as dirty as these men were.
>
> — H.G. Bissinger, *Friday Night Lights*, 1990

[Perhaps from Low German *oghelen, oegeln*, to ogle, from *oegen*, to eye, from *oghe, oge*, eye, akin to English *eye*, High German *Auge*.]

ostentatious (ŏs′tĕn-tā′shəs)

adjective

Characterized by showiness meant to impress others;
pretentious in display.

> "That Porsche," someone on my right said, "is one nice
> ride. Sixty-six?"
>
> "Sixty-three," I said and turned to look at him.
>
> Pine wore a camel hair topcoat and burgundy twill
> trousers and a black cashmere sweater. His black gloves
> looked like a second skin over his hands.
>
> "How'd you afford it?" he said.
>
> "I pretty much bought a body only," I said. "Acquired
> parts over several years."
>
> "You one of those guys who loves his car more than
> his wife or friends?"
>
> I held up the keys. "It's chrome and metal and rubber,
> Pine, and it couldn't mean less to me right now. You want
> it, take it."
>
> He shook his head. "Far too **ostentatious** for my
> tastes. Drive an Acura myself."
>
> — Dennis Lehane, *Darkness, Take My Hand*, 1996

[From Latin *ostentāre*, to show off, from *ostendere*, to show.]

Even in the darkness of the car, with only the intermittent streetlights to give it life, the diamond was overwhelming.

She shrank away. "I can't take that!"

"Don't you like it?"

"Like it! It's the most fantastic thing I've ever seen!"

"Ten karats," he said easily. "But in a square cut it's not at all **ostentatious**."

"Of course not," she laughed nervously. "Every secretary has one."

— Jacqueline Susann,
Valley of the Dolls, 1966

ostracize (ŏs′trə-sīz′)

verb

To exclude from a group.

> But the long-term deterrent of spreading our ideals throughout the world is just not enough, and may never be realized, if we do not act — and act together — to remove the clear and present danger posed by terrorism and terrorists. The United Nations must hold accountable any country that supports or condones terrorism, otherwise you will fail in your primary mission as peacekeeper. It must **ostracize** any nation that supports terrorism.

> — Rudy Giuliani, Opening Remarks to the United Nations General Assembly, Special Session on Terrorism, October 1, 2001

> Desperate for a nightly fix for talking heads, some stations sign talent for hefty fees. . . . But "expertification," as The Street.com's James Cramer calls it, has its price. Viewers want to argue with you when you're waiting to buy groceries. Your peers may **ostracize** you for selling out. And as with everything on network television, you have to break down your analysis to its lowest common denominator.

> — Erika Brown, "Hired Heads," *Forbes*, March 22, 1999

[From Greek *ostrakizein*, from *ostrakon*, shell, potsherd (from the potsherds used in ancient Greece as ballots in voting to ostracize a person).]

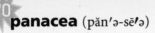

panacea (păn′ə-sē′ə)

noun

A remedy for all diseases, evils, or difficulties; a cure-all.

> All right, I'm not a union organizer any more than I'm Wal-Mart "management material," as Isabelle has hinted. In fact, I don't share the belief, held by many union staffers, that unionization would be a **panacea**. Sure, almost any old union would boost wages and straighten out some backbones here, but I know that even the most energetic and democratic unions bear careful watching by their members.
>
> — Barbara Ehrenreich, *Nickel and Dimed: On (Not) Getting By in America*, 2001

> The first **panacea** for a mismanaged nation is inflation of the currency; the second is war. Both bring a temporary prosperity; both bring a permanent ruin. But both are the refuge of political and economic opportunists.
>
> — Ernest Hemingway, "Notes on the Next War: A Serious Topical Letter," *Esquire*, September 1935

[Latin *panacēa*, from Greek *panakeia*, from *panakēs*, all-healing : *pan-*, all + *akos*, cure.]

paradox (păr′ə-dŏks)

noun

1. A statement that seems to contradict itself but that may nonetheless be true. **2.** A person or thing that is apparently contradictory or has conflicting aspects.

> The students were hiding inside the music, inside their technique, and Ms. Cook set about dragging them out and making them lay bare their own truths, even if it meant awkwardness, embarrassment and some blunt criticism — leavened, in all cases, by sincerely delivered hugs and kisses. She put forth a telling **paradox**: "The place that seems most dangerous is exactly where safety lies." In other words, self-exposure and the abandonment of technical propriety, scary as it was, was the surest, the best, maybe the only way to communicate with an audience.
>
> — Charles Isherwood, "Take Off Your Emotional Clothes and Sing," *New York Times*, December 11, 2005

> The United States can achieve its full economic and social potential as a nation only if every individual has the opportunity to contribute to the full extent of his capabilities and to participate in the workings of our society. It is, therefore, the policy of the United States to eliminate the **paradox** of poverty in the midst of plenty in this Nation by opening to everyone the opportunity for education and training, the opportunity to work, and the opportunity to live in decency and dignity.
>
> — The Economic Opportunity Act, quoted by President Lyndon Johnson, State of the Union Address, January 14, 1969

[From Latin *paradoxum*, from Greek *paradoxon*, from neuter singular of *paradoxos*, conflicting with expectation : *para-*, beyond + *doxa*, opinion (from *dokein*, to think).]

peevish (pē′vĭsh)

adjective

Discontented or irritable.

> In the past it had galled the Bishop to see the King being corrected by his wife, but now he perceived that Henry himself was becoming irritated with her arguments. Encroaching infirmity made him **peevish** and impatient; he ceased making his daily visits to his wife's apartments, and it was left to Katherine to decide whether or not to brave his black moods and go and sit with him after dinner or supper.
>
> — B. Alison Weir, *Six Wives of Henry VIII,* 1991

> Joseph was an elderly, ay, an old man: very old, perhaps, though hale and sinewy. "The Lord help us!" he soliloquized in an undertone of **peevish** displeasure, while relieving me of my horse: looking, meantime, in my face so sourly that I charitably conjectured he must have need of divine aid to digest his dinner.
>
> — Emily Brontë, *Wuthering Heights*, 1847

[Middle English *pevish*, possibly from Latin *perversus*, past participle of *pervertere*, to pervert : *per-*, thoroughly + *vertere*, to turn.]

perfunctory (pər-fŭngk′tə-rē)

adjective

Done routinely and with little interest or care.

> Reforms in the civil service must go on; but the changes should be real and genuine, not **perfunctory**, or prompted by a zeal in behalf of any party simply because it happens to be in power.
>
> — President William McKinley, First Inaugural Address, March 4, 1897

> Her rapid footsteps shook her own floors, and she routed lassitude and indifference wherever she came. She could not be negative or **perfunctory** about anything. Her enthusiasm, and her violent likes and dislikes, asserted themselves in all the everyday occupations of life.
>
> — Willa Cather, *My Ántonia*, 1918

[Late Latin *perfūnctōrius,* from Latin *perfūnctus,* past participle of *perfungī,* to get through with : *per-,* through + *fungī,* to perform.]

philistine *also* **Philistine** (fĭl′ĭ-stēn′)

noun

A person who is smugly indifferent or antagonistic to art and culture.

adjective

Displaying or characterized by the attitudes of a philistine.

> Throughout her career, [Edith] Wharton had to contend with **Philistines** who thought her fiction sordid or immoral, and sometimes she condescended to write not what she knew to be good and demanding work, but commercial fare acceptable to editors.
>
> — Peter S. Prescott, "Portrait of a Lady,"
> *Newsweek*, September 22, 1975

> Now libraries devote far too much of their restricted space, and their limited budget, to public amusement. It is a fact of **philistine** life that amusement is where the money is.
>
> Universities attract students by promising them, on behalf of their parents, a happy present and a comfortable future, and these intentions are passed along through the system like salmonella until budgets are cut, research requirements are skimped, and the fundamental formula for academic excellence is ignored if not forgotten.
>
> — William H. Gass, "In Defense of the Book,"
> *Harper's Magazine*, November 1999

[From Middle English *Philistines*, Philistines, from Late Latin *Philistīnī*, from Greek *Philistīnoi*, from Hebrew *Pəlištîm*, from *Pəlešet*, Philistia.]

The Philistines were a people of the ancient Near East who lived in Philistia, the coastal area in and around what is now called the Gaza Strip. The Bible depicts them in a struggle with the tribes of Israel for ascendancy in the region. The mighty Israelite warrior Samson, for example, fought with the Philistines on several occasions, even though he married a Philistine woman. Samson also fell in love with another Philistine woman, Delilah, who proved to be his undoing. While Samson slept in her lap, Delilah had the locks of hair that gave Samson his superhuman strength shaved off, and his Philistine enemies were able to capture and enslave him.

The most common modern meaning of the word, "a smugly ignorant and uncultured person," is said to stem from a memorial service given in 1693 for a student killed during a town-gown quarrel in Jena, a university town in Germany. The minister preached a sermon from the text *Philister über dir Simson!* ("The Philistines be upon thee, Samson!"), Delilah's words to Samson after she attempted to render him powerless before the Philistines. German students came to use *Philister,* the German equivalent of the English word *Philistine,* to refer to nonstudents and hence uncultured or materialistic people, and this usage was picked up in English in the early 19th century.

precocious (prĭ-kō′shəs)

adjective

Displaying or characterized by unusually early development or maturity, especially in intelligence.

> Think about Richard Scarry's *Cars and Trucks and Things That Go*. Think about what that book would have looked like in sequential decades of the last century had Richard Scarry been alive in each of them to delight and amuse children and parents. . . . We started with the model-T Ford. We now have more models of backhoe loaders than even the most **precocious** four-year-old can identify.
>
> — George A. Akerlof, Nobel Lecture, December 8, 2001

> Blind children, it has often been noted, tend to be **precocious** verbally, and may develop such fluency in the verbal description of faces and places as to leave others (and perhaps themselves) uncertain as to whether they are actually blind.
>
> — Oliver Sacks, "The Mind's Eye: What the Blind See," *The New Yorker*, July 28, 2003

[From Latin *praecox, praecoc-*, premature, from *praecoquere*, to boil before, ripen early : *prae-*, before + *coquere*, to cook, ripen.]

propriety (prə-prī′ĭ-tē)

noun

Conformity to prevailing customs and usages.

The greatest outburst of prudery came in the nineteenth century when it swept through the world like a fever. It was an age when sensibilities grew so delicate that one lady was reported to have dressed her goldfish in miniature suits for the sake of **propriety** and a certain Madame de la Bresse left her fortune to provide clothing for the snowmen of Paris.

— Bill Bryson, *The Mother Tongue*, 1990

ELIZABETH [*Descending the staircase*]: Will! It's so good to see you! I had a dream about you last night.

WILL: About me?

SWANN [*Flustered*]: Is that entirely proper for you to ...?

ELIZABETH [*Ignoring her father*]: About the day we met. Do you remember?

WILL: How could I forget, Miss Swann?

ELIZABETH: Will, how many times must I ask you to call me Elizabeth?

WILL: At least once more, Miss Swann. As always.

[*Elizabeth is disappointed.*]

SWANN: There, you see, at least the boy has a sense of **propriety**! Now, we really must be going.

— from the film *Pirates of the Caribbean: The Curse of the Black Pearl*, 2003

[From Middle English *propriete*, particular character, ownership, from Old French, from Latin *proprietās*, from *proprius*, one's own.]

quid pro quo (kwĭd′ prō kwō′)

noun

Plural: **quid pro quos** or **quids pro quo**

Something given in return for something else or accepted as a reciprocal part of an exchange.

> Lothian now cabled that Mr. Sumner Welles had told him that the constitutional position made it "utterly impossible" for the President to send the destroyers as a spontaneous gift; they could come only as a **quid pro quo**.
>
> —Winston S. Churchill, *The Second World War, Volume II: Their Finest Hour*, 1949

> I read with appreciation one editorial after another . . . excoriating the soft-money binges, the lavish fund-raisers, the Niagara of money pouring into both major party coffers at countless events stamped by corporate logos. The press named names of fat-cat companies and what the expected **quid pro quos** were from the politicians.
>
> —Ralph Nader, *Crashing the Party: Taking on the Corporate Government in an Age of Surrender*, 2002

[From Latin *quid prō quō* : *quid*, something + *prō*, for + *quō*, ablative form of *quid*, something.]

quintessential (kwĭn′tə-sĕn′shəl)

adjective

Being the best or most typical example of its kind.

> Harry Truman and the pearl gray Stetson and the light gray suit and the round-rimmed glasses and the walking stick. Harry Truman on his morning stroll, the brisk cadence of his walk matched by the blunt rhythm of his speech. Plain spoken, plain talking, no nonsense Harry. Little Harry, some people called him when he first took Roosevelt's place. Little man, they called him, the day FDR died. Funny that little Harry looms so large in our memories. He was in many ways the **quintessential** American.
>
> — President Ronald Reagan, from the TV show
> *The MacNeil/Lehrer NewsHour*, May 8, 1984

> I spent eight years talking to the astronauts and many of the other people who worked with them. And I have to tell you that even now — and I keep meeting people from other phases of the program — I still can't comprehend Apollo. It is just such a vast undertaking. And to me that is really the impact of it, that it stands as probably the **quintessential** story of human cooperation and ingenuity — the fact that people were able to band together . . . not only to accomplish something that seemed like science fiction but to do it with a deadline, and it was a truly remarkable period in our history.
>
> — Andrew Chaiken, space historian, from the TV
> show *The NewsHour with Jim Lehrer*,
> July 20, 1999

[From Middle English, from Old French *quinte essence*, fifth essence, from Medieval Latin *quīnta essentia* (translation of Greek *pemptē ousiā*) : Latin *quīnta*, feminine of *quīntus*, fifth + Latin *essentia*, essence.]

In contemporary English, the noun *quintessence* is most often used to mean "the purest or most typical instance." The term originates, in fact, in the earliest speculation about the nature of existence by Western philosophers. In the fifth and fourth centuries BC, Greek philosophers engaged in a lively debate about the ultimate composition of physical matter, a debate that helped lay the foundations of the Western philosophical tradition. The early philosopher Empedocles (ca. 490–ca. 430 BC) held the view that the universe was made up of four elements—earth, air, fire, and water—and that these elements were acted upon by two principles, which he called Love and Strife. Plato (427–ca. 347 BC) and Aristotle (384–322 BC) later discussed the existence of a fifth element, of which the heavens were thought to be composed. This fifth element was usually called *aithēr*, a word that originally referred to the heavens as the brilliant dwelling place of the gods and the realm of the stars and planets.

The root of this term, *aith-*, can be found in many other Greek words referring to the notion of bright light, such as *aithops*, "flashing, fiery," and *aithra*, "cloudless sky." Besides being the element of the sky, *aithēr* was also thought to be distributed throughout earthly objects and to contribute to their cohesion. Later followers of Aristotle began using the term *pemptē ousiā*, "fifth element," for *aithēr*. Medieval European alchemists and scientists translated the Greek phrase into Latin as *quīnta essentia*, and the Latin expression entered English as *quintessence*. As part of their investigations into the nature of matter, alchemists sought to isolate the heavenly quintessence from the other four base elements by elaborate procedures of refinement and distillation, and from their attempts, the word *quintessence* came to mean "the pure, highly concentrated essence of a thing." *Quintessential* is the corresponding adjective.

red herring

noun

Something that draws attention away from the matter at hand.

> Teachers complained it took weeks to get these mandatory plays ready, weeks that would be better spent on lessons to bring up the school's repeated dreadful showings on standardized tests. But Mrs. Scalise dismissed that as a **red herring**, pointing out the extra time wouldn't help a poor teacher improve test scores.
>
> — Sam Swope, *I Am a Pencil: A Teacher, His Kids, and Their World of Stories*, 2004

A red herring was originally a herring cured by smoking, a process that imparted a reddish color to its flesh. Because of its strong fishy smell, the herring was sometimes considered poor-quality food and associated with poverty and deprivation. Nevertheless, smoked red herrings were a dietary staple throughout northern Europe well into early modern times.

How did this fish become associated with a distraction in an argument? It is not known exactly, but probably by way of hunting. A hunting guide published in the 1600s recommends dragging a red herring along the ground to create a scent trail so that hounds and horses can get exercise on days when a real quarry cannot be scared up. It may be that the modern meaning of the word developed from the notion of deliberately laying an artificial trail to be tracked by the hounds. In any event, in the 19th century, the idea of a "false lead" became associated with the odorous fish, and *red herring* was used metaphorically to describe intriguing but irrelevant trains of thought.

In the Hiss case they [the Russians] got the secrets which enabled them to break the American secret State Department code. They got secrets in the atomic bomb case which enabled them to get the secret of the atomic bomb five years before they would have gotten it by their own devices. And I say that any man who called the Alger Hiss case a **red herring** isn't fit to be President of the United States.

— President Richard M. Nixon, Checkers speech, September 23, 1952

80 revel (rĕv′əl)

verb

To take great pleasure or delight in something.

> Archaeologists **revel** in contradictions, **revel** in a feeling that something should not be and might even be impossible, but somehow is. We all love a good mystery. It's what keeps us in the field. It's what keeps the field honest.
>
> — Charles Pellegrino, *Ghosts of the Titanic*, 2000

> These days, in fact, it's usually only entertainers and celebrities who unapologetically **revel** in being rich, mindful of their obligation to live out the fantasies of the rest of us. "My God is a God who wants me to have things," Mary J. Blige recently told *Blender* magazine. "He wants me to bling."
>
> — Geoffrey Nunberg, "An Adjective for Cakes, But Not for Bill Gates," *New York Times*, April 30, 2006

[From Middle English *revelen*, to carouse, from Old French *reveler*, to rebel, carouse, from Latin *rebellāre*, to rebel : *re-*, against, opposite + *bellāre*, to make war (from *bellum*, war).]

rhetoric (rĕt'ər-ĭk)

noun

Language that is intended to persuade, especially when viewed as pretentious, insincere, or without intellectual merit.

> He just borrowed me for a while when he came to Newark, occasionally borrowed me to have somebody to talk to when he was lonely visiting Newark or by himself up at the shack, but never took me anywhere near a Communist meeting. That whole other life of his was almost entirely invisible to me. All I got was the rant and the raving and the **rhetoric**, the window dressing.
>
> — Philip Roth, *I Married a Communist*, 1998

> Our culture is fascinated by the rich and the young, and elite boarding schools are a place where the two intersect. . . . It's not that I see boarding schools as evil. I just don't see them as necessary, and despite their often self-congratulatory **rhetoric**, I don't see them as noble — certainly no more so than public schools.
>
> — Curtis Sittenfeld, "Parental Supervision Required," *New York Times*, September 7, 2005

[Ultimately from Latin *rhētoricē, rhētorica*, from Greek *rhētorikē (tekhnē)*, rhetorical (art), feminine of *rhētorikos*, rhetorical, from *rhētōr*, rhetor.]

In the ancient world, because public speaking was so important in advancing one's own cause as well as the general good, the teaching of public speaking, known as *rhetoric*, became very important and highlighted the devices used to make an effective speech. Because the teachers of rhetoric could make at least a superficial case for almost any argument, regardless of its true merit, some people regarded them as amoral. Thus, even in ancient times rhetoric could have a bad reputation, and that reputation has persisted today.

scintillating (sĭn′tl-ā′tĭng)

adjective

Lively and exceptionally intelligent; animated and brilliant.

> DAVID: How 'bout if you help me, unless I'm horning in here.
>
> SOFIA: You are, but the food's good.
>
> DAVID: I have a problem. I got a stalker.
>
> SOFIA: It doesn't sound life-threatening.
>
> DAVID: But I need a cover. I need for you to pretend we are having a **scintillating** conversation, and you are wildly entertained. I know it's tough.
>
> SOFIA: I'll improvise.
>
> — from the film *Vanilla Sky*, 2001

[From Latin *scintillāre, scintillāt-*, to sparkle, from *scintilla*, spark.]

During the four hours of oral argument a day — from ten in the morning until three in the afternoon, with an hour's break for lunch — the justices often amused themselves by passing notes commenting either on the courtroom proceedings or on events in the wider world. The days were long, not every argument was **scintillating**, and attention sometimes flagged. "Bill — You have been utterly quiet today! Is everything all right?" Blackmun asked in a note to Brennan. "I'm just bored. The previous argument was atrocious," Brennan replied.

— Linda Greenhouse, *Becoming Justice Blackmun: Harry Blackmun's Supreme Court Journey,* 2005

spartan *also* **Spartan** (spär′tn)

adjective

1. Rigorously self-disciplined or self-restrained. **2.** Having a simple or severe manner or appearance.

> I've been in football all my life, really, and I want to say this — that it's a great game, and it's a **spartan** type of game. I mean by that, it takes **spartan** qualities in order to be a part of it, to play it. And I speak of the **spartan** qualities of sacrifice and self-denial rather than that other **spartan** quality of leaving the weak to die.
>
> —Vince Lombardi, audio recording posted at www.rhetoric.com

> The nation itself, with all its so-called internal improvements, which, by the way are all external and superficial, is just such an unwieldy and overgrown establishment, cluttered with furniture and tripped up by its own traps, ruined by luxury and heedless expense, by want of calculation and a worthy aim, as the million households in the land; and the only cure for it, as for them, is in a rigid economy, a stern and more than **Spartan** simplicity of life and elevation of purpose. It lives too fast.
>
> —Henry David Thoreau, *Walden*, 1854

[From Latin *Spartānus,* from Greek *Sparta, Spartē,* Sparta.]

In ancient times, the military prowess of Sparta allowed it to vie with Athens for the domination of Greece. In order to maintain a martial spirit, the Spartan upper classes endured a regimented life whose rigor was as much a source of amazement to their fellow Greeks as it is to us today. When an infant was born in an upper-class Spartan family, the community elders would examine it, and if they found it to possess any defects, it would be thrown over a cliff. At the age of seven, boys left their families to live in communal barracks, where they were drilled in military exercises. They slept on reeds they plucked with their bare hands, and they had one piece of clothing, a cloak of wool that they wore, rain or shine, throughout the year. They were deliberately underfed and encouraged to steal food, in order to learn the skill of approaching the enemy in secret.

At the age of twenty, the young men were admitted to the communal dining halls where all male citizens were obliged to take their meals. There they ate simple foods that kept them fit and ready for battle, such as barley, cheese, figs, watered wine, and pork seasoned with just salt and vinegar. Exceptionally among the ancient Greeks, women as well as men were given a good education so that they could serve the city by raising children who would be devoted to Spartan goals.

The rough training and regimented lifestyle produced an elite corps of soldiers that enabled Sparta to dominate much of Greece from the 6th to the middle of the 4th century BC, when Spartan power entered a decline. The austere life of the Spartan people is still remembered today when English speakers use the adjective *spartan* to describe a frugal meal or a very simple lifestyle.

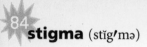

stigma (stĭg′mə)

noun

An association of disgrace or public disapproval with a characteristic, condition, or behavior.

> You are all on fire at the mention of liberty for France or for Ireland, but are as cold as an iceberg at the thought of liberty for the enslaved of America. You discourse eloquently on the dignity of labor; yet, you sustain a system which, in its very essence, casts a **stigma** upon labor. You can bare your bosom to the storm of British artillery to throw off a threepenny tax on tea, and yet wring the last hard-earned farthing from the grasp of the black laborers of your country.
>
> — Frederick Douglass, "What to the Slave is the Fourth of July?" speech, July 5, 1852

> Despite the fact that major depression ranks second only to heart disease in the nation's "disease burden" (a measure that takes both mortality and morbidity into account), and despite the great scientific leaps that psychiatry has made, the report found the **stigma** associated with mental illness to be overwhelming: many people do not even accept that mental function is the work of a physical organ — a basic tenet of psychiatry.
>
> — Daniel Smith, "Shock and Disbelief," *The Atlantic Monthly*, February 2001

[From Middle English *stigme*, mark of infamy, wound received by Jesus during the crucifixion, from Latin *stigma*, *stigmat-*, tattoo indicating slave or criminal status, from Greek, tattoo mark, from *stizein*, *stig-*, to prick.]

stoic *also* **Stoic** (stō′ĭk)

adjective

Seemingly indifferent to pleasure and pain; showing little or no emotion.

> Of all the American women who wrote diaries in the eighteenth century, Mary [Cooper] is unique in that she constantly complained. Colonists were a **stoic** lot, experts at repressing emotion or throwing all their woes into the lap of a hopefully benevolent Deity. But Mary didn't withhold. "O I am tired almost to death," was one of her favorite refrains.
>
> — Gail Collins, *America's Women: Four Hundred Years of Dolls, Drudges, Helpmates, and Heroines*, 2003

> There are two ways of coping with fear: one is to diminish the external danger, and the other is to cultivate **Stoic** endurance.
>
> — Bertrand Russell, Nobel Lecture, December 11, 1950

[From Middle English *Stoic*, a Stoic, from Latin *Stōicus*, from Greek *Stōikos*, from *Stoā Poikilē*, Painted Stoa, name of a building in Athens where Zeno of Citium, the founder of Stoicism, taught.]

The Stoic school of philosophy was founded by the Greek philosopher Zeno of Citium during the late 4th century BC. Zeno taught in a building in Athens called the Stoa Poikile, "the Painted Stoa." A *stoa* is a covered walk or colonnade, usually having columns on one side and a wall on the other. The Stoa Poikile itself was named for the painted panels of battle scenes that adorned its wall. Since Zeno's followers would gather in the Stoa Poikile to discuss philosophy, they came to be called "the Stoics." They believed that a transcendent being had created the universe and ordered it according to reason. Since this being had established natural principles for the best, the Stoics thought that a life lived in accordance with nature and reason and embodying qualities like courage, justice, and temperance was sufficient for happiness. Stoicism continued to flourish in Roman times, when Stoics advocated the calm acceptance of all circumstances as the unavoidable result of divine will or the natural order. Such attitudes eventually led to the use of *stoic* and *stoical* to describe people who seem indifferent to both pleasure and pain.

86

suave (swäv)

adjective

Gracious and sophisticated.

> CHESSY: Look, you and I both know your father's not some kind of **suave**, debonair bachelor-of-the-month type, so I got to ask myself what does a young hot thing like that see in a guy who walks around with his shirttail hanging out and his cereal bowl full of chili. Then I realized, there's about a million reasons why that girl's giggling, and all of them are sitting at the Napa Valley Community Bank.
>
> — from the film *The Parent Trap*, 1998

> Instead of [Cary] Grant or Fred Astaire playing **suave** playboys, we have Quentin Tarantino's cool-cat killers and hit men, we have Anthony Hopkins's ingratiating Hannibal the Cannibal in "The Silence of the Lambs" and a charmingly cynical John Travolta in "Broken Arrow," sexily vowing to blow Southwestern America back to the Stone Age.
>
> — Michiko Kakutani, "Designer Nihilism,"
> *New York Times*, March 24, 1996

[From French *suave*, agreeable, from Old French, from Latin *suāvis*, delightful, sweet.]

Svengali (svĕn-gä′lē)

noun

A person who manipulates or controls another for malicious purposes, especially by force of personality.

> ED: But in front of the jury they had it that Doris was a saint; the whole plan had been mine, I was a **Svengali** who'd forced Doris to join my criminal enterprise.
>
> — from the film *The Man Who Wasn't There*, 2001

> [Sydney] Carroll was a man of conceit and power, something of a **Svengali** in London theatrical management since he liked to assume total influence over those he put under contract.
>
> — Alexander Walker, *Vivien: A Life of Vivien Leigh*, 1989

[After *Svengali*, the hypnotist villain in the novel *Trilby* by George du Maurier (1834–1896).]

George du Maurier's novel *Trilby*, set in bohemian Paris of the 1850s, was enormously popular after its publication in 1894. The villain of the novel, the sinister hypnotist Svengali, uses his hypnotic powers to enslave a tone-deaf young woman named Trilby O'Ferrall and transform her into a magnificent singer. Svengali conducts her concerts and lives in luxury off the earnings from Trilby's performances. When Svengali dies from a heart attack at the beginning of a concert, Trilby awakens from her trance completely unable to sing or even remember what has happened to her. The audience hoots her from the stage and she dies soon after, unable to survive outside the influence of the hypnotic power of her cruel master. The 1931 film *Svengali*, starring John Barrymore as the title character, helped make Svengali even more notorious.

sycophant (sĭk′ə-fənt *or* sī′kə-fənt)

noun

A person who attempts to gain advantage by flattering influential people or behaving in a submissive way.

> In the world in which we live today, a lawyer without any enemies is likely to be a coward and a **sycophant**. A lawyer with the right enemies is often an advocate who has taken on powerful interests and stood up for the poor, the disenfranchised and the despised.
>
> —Alan Dershowitz, *Letters to a Young Lawyer*, 2001

> For a kid who had been raised on tales of the GI generation's heroic accomplishments, it was obvious that our civilization was in decay, that we had gotten too far away from the natural order of things. As anyone could see from the movies, America was rotten with **sycophants** and dope and processed foods and entire classes of public hangers-on.
>
> —Thomas Frank, *What's the Matter with Kansas? How Conservatives Won the Heart of America*, 2004

[From Latin *sȳcophanta*, informer, slanderer, from Greek *sūkophantēs*, informer, from *sūkon phainein*, to show a fig (probably originally said of denouncers of theft or exportation of figs, whose export from Athens was forbidden) : *sūkon*, fig + *phainein*, to show.]

teetotaler *or* teetotaller (tē'tōt'l-ər)

noun

One who abstains completely from alcoholic beverages.

> If I'd been a **teetotaler** those guys in the legislature would have driven me to drink.
>
> — Ronald Reagan, from a 1971 letter in *Reagan: A Life in Letters*, edited by Kiron K. Skinner et al., 2003

> [Spencer] Tracy, who was within a few weeks of starting the ill-fated *Tribute to a Bad Man*, was on the wagon so diligently that Hemingway thought he was a **teetotaler**.
>
> — Anne Edwards, *Katharine Hepburn: A Remarkable Woman*, 1985

[Probably partly from *tee* (pronunciation of the first letter in *total*) + *total* (*abstinence*), and partly reduplication of *total*.]

tête-à-tête (tāt′ə-tāt′ *or* tĕt′ə-tĕt′)

noun

A private conversation between two people.

> Among the musical people he frequented, he found himself on a callow kind of equality with everybody, even the stars and aristocrats, at one moment, and a backstairs outsider the next. It was all just as the moment demanded. There was a certain excitement in slithering up and down the social scale, one minute chatting in a personal **tête-à-tête** with the most famous, or notorious, of the society beauties: and the next walking in the rain, with his flute in a bag, to his grubby lodging in Bloomsbury.

— D.H. Lawrence, *Aaron's Rod*, 1922

> Spennie hesitated for an instant when he saw who was in the room. He was not over-anxious for a **tête-à-tête** with Molly's father just then. But, reflecting that, after all, he was not to blame for any disappointment that might be troubling the other, he switched on his grin again, and walked in.

— P.G. Wodehouse, *The Intrusion of Jimmy*, 1910

[From French *tête-à-tête* : *tête*, head + *à*, to + *tête*, head.]

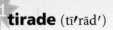

tirade (tī′rād′)

noun

A long, angry speech, usually of a critical nature.

> MOLLY: Do you know what étage your daughter's at in bal-
> let, Mrs. Schleine? Or that she was banned from her
> science class for stealing a formaldehyde pig so that
> she could give it a proper burial in Central Park? And
> the tea set you got her, it's exquisite and beautiful,
> but do you know how she likes to have her tea — how
> many lumps, one lump, two . . . cream, sugar?
> MRS. SCHLEINE: And the point of your little **tirade** is . . .
> MOLLY: You're right. You don't know what goes on be-
> tween me and Ray because you don't know very
> much about your own daughter.
>
> — from the film *Uptown Girls*, 2003

> When Velutha arrived, Mammachi lost her bearings and
> spewed her blind venom, her crass, insufferable
> insults . . . at Velutha standing very still in the gloom.
> Mammachi continued her **tirade**, her eyes empty, her
> face twisted and ugly, her anger propelling her towards
> Velutha until she was shouting right into his face and he
> could feel the spray of her spit and smell the stale tea on
> her breath.
>
> — Arundhati Roy, *The God of Small Things*, 1997

[French, from Old French, act of firing, from *tirer,* to draw out, endure, probably back-formation from *martirant,* present participle of *martirer,* to torture (influenced by *mar,* to one's detriment, and *tiranz,* executioner, tyrant), from *martir,* martyr, from Late Latin *martyr,* from Late Greek *martur,* from Greek *martus, martur-,* witness (as to the Christian faith).]

tryst (trĭst)

noun

1. An agreement, as between lovers, to meet at a certain time and place. **2.** A meeting or meeting place that has been agreed on.

> Long years ago we made a **tryst** with destiny, and now the time comes when we shall redeem our pledge, not wholly or in full measure, but very substantially. At the stroke of the midnight hour, when the world sleeps, India will awake to life and freedom.
>
> — Jawaharlal Nehru, speech given to the Constituent Assembly, New Delhi, August 14, 1947

> You want to go directly across the street to Bergdorf's Men's Shop on Fifth Avenue, but the Plaza fountain is directly in your path, with people from all walks of life sitting on the ledge of the fountain, eating sandwiches in what's left of their lunch hour, talking to their friends from the office, maybe flirting with some new acquaintance and whispering arrangements for a love **tryst** that night.
>
> — Gene Wilder, *Kiss Me Like a Stranger: My Search for Love and Art*, 2005

[From Middle English *trist*, from Old French *triste*, a waiting place (in hunting).]

ubiquitous (yōo-bĭk′wĭ-təs)

adjective

Being or seeming to be everywhere at the same time.

Schubert lived a mere 31 years, yet composed well over a thousand works, a prodigy who wrote music faster than most people can transcribe it. Today his themes are top-40 famous, at least to classical buffs. The "Impromptu" in B-flat major; the **ubiquitous** "Ave Maria"; the "Unfinished Symphony." But in Schubert's day almost nothing was published or even publicly performed.

— Paul Solman, from the TV show *The NewsHour with Jim Lehrer*, February 25, 1997

One of the wild suggestings referred to, as at last coming to be linked with the white whale in the minds of the superstitiously inclined, was the unearthly conceit that Moby Dick was **ubiquitous**; that he had actually been encountered in opposite latitudes at one and the same instant of time.

— Herman Melville, *Moby-Dick*, 1851

[From New Latin *ubīquitās*, from Latin *ubīque*, everywhere : *ubī*, where + -*que*, and (also appended to other words to give them a generalizing sense).]

unrequited (ŭn-rĭ-kwī′tĭd)

adjective

Not given, rewarded, or felt in return.

> To highlight the isolation and unfamiliar surroundings, the manuals instruct the police to display an air of confidence in the suspect's guilt and from outward appearance to maintain only an interest in confirming certain details. The guilt of the subject is to be posited as a fact. The interrogator should direct his comments toward the reasons why the subject committed the act, rather than court failure by asking the subject whether he did it. Like other men, perhaps the subject has had a bad family life, had an unhappy childhood, had too much to drink, had an **unrequited** desire for women. The officers are instructed to minimize the moral seriousness of the offense, to cast blame on the victim or on society. These tactics are designed to put the subject in a psychological state where his story is but an elaboration of what the police purport to know already—that he is guilty. Explanations to the contrary are dismissed and discouraged.
>
> — Chief Justice Earl Warren, US Supreme Court,
> *Miranda v. Arizona*, 384 US 436 (1966)

MAXINE: I've fallen in love.

CRAIG: I don't think so. You know why? Because I've fallen in love! And this is what people who've fallen in love look like!

MAXINE: You picked the **unrequited** variety. It's very bad for the skin.

> — from the film *Being John Malkovich*, 1999

[From *un-*, not + *requited*, past participle of *requite*, to repay.]

Fondly do we hope, fervently do we pray, that this mighty scourge of war may speedily pass away. Yet, if God wills that it continue until all the wealth piled by the bondsman's two hundred and fifty years of **unrequited** toil shall be sunk, and until every drop of blood drawn with the lash shall be paid by another drawn with the sword, as was said three thousand years ago, so still it must be said "the judgments of the Lord are true and righteous altogether."

— President Abraham Lincoln, Second Inaugural Address, March 4, 1865

95

untenable (ŭn-tĕn′ə-bəl)

adjective

1. Impossible to maintain or defend, as against criticism. **2.** Impossible to tolerate or endure.

> Gentlemen of the jury, whatever your verdict will be, as far as we are concerned, nothing will be changed. I have held ideas all my life. I have publicly held my ideas for twenty-seven years. Nothing on earth would ever make me change my ideas except one thing; and that is, if you will prove to me that our position is wrong, **untenable**, or lacking in historic fact. But never would I change my ideas because I am found guilty.
>
> — Emma Goldman, Address to the Jury,
>   July 9, 1917

> The waters have been shifting constantly within the city itself. Some areas that were dry last night, people woke up this morning and found that they had been surrounded by water. In other words, what was a bad situation, by sunrise, had become almost an **untenable** situation.
>
> — Martin Savidge, from the TV show *Hardball with Chris Matthews*, August 31, 2005

[From *un-*, not + *tenable,* from French, from Old French, from *tenir,* to hold, from Latin *tenēre.*]

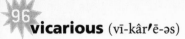

96

vicarious (vī-kâr′ē-əs)

adjective

Experienced or felt by empathy with or imaginary participation in the life of another person.

> The debate on the House floor is still droning on, and while Democrats grumble over the long hours, nothing can dampen the exuberance of the Republicans, as vote tally after vote tally confirms the new reality. They're actually winning, and they want to keep doing it even if it takes all night. . . . This afternoon, their side of the House aisle was crowded with former members who had come back to the scene of so many defeats for, at last, a day of **vicarious** victory.
>
> — Cokie Roberts, from the TV show *Nightline*, January 4, 1995

[From Latin *vicārius*, vicarious, a substitute, from *vicis*, genitive form of **vix*, change.]

97

vile (vīl)

adjective

1. Loathsome, disgusting. **2.** Morally depraved or wicked.

> When I tasted it I knew why. It had been another of Pinky's cost-cutting measures, her replacing the local honey with the Chinese honey that came in five-gallon pails and was poured into squirt bottles. This stuff was **vile**, with the dusty oversweet industrial taste of the Chinese corn syrup that had been used to adulterate it.
>
> — Paul Theroux, *Hotel Honolulu*, 2001

> PATRICK: So what's up with your dad? Is he a pain in the ass?
> KAT: No. He just wants me to be someone I'm not.
> PATRICK: Who?
> KAT: Bianca.
> PATRICK: Ah . . . Bianca. No offense or anything, I mean, I know everyone digs your sister. But, um . . . She's without . . .
> KAT: You know, you're not as **vile** as I thought you were.
>
> — from the film *10 Things I Hate About You*, 1999

[From Middle English *vile,* from Old French, from Latin *vīlis,* cheap, worthless.]

---

waft (wäft *or* wăft)

verb

To move or cause to move gently and smoothly through the air.

> He had a straight chair where he would go to sit some-times and stare out the window over at the high school, listen for the sound of band practice **wafting** over from the field, but mostly he spent his hours in the back on the first floor, in the kitchen building dollhouses, in the living room listening to the radio . . .
>
> —Alice Sebold, *The Lovely Bones*, 2002

> The weather of the world remained fair, and the wind held in the west, but nothing could **waft** away the glooms and the sad mists that clung about the Mountains of Shadow; and behind them at whiles great smokes would arise and hover in the upper winds.
>
> —J.R.R. Tolkien, *The Lord of the Rings: The Return of the King*, 1955

[From earlier *waft*, to convoy, back-formation from *wafter*, convoy ship, alteration of Middle English *waughter*, from Middle Dutch, or Middle Low German *wachter*, a guard, from *wachten*, to guard.]

white elephant

noun

A possession that is burdensome to or unwanted by its owner.

> One of the very first things Mimi had done was to orga-
> nize the purchase of the old Wannamaker estate in East
> Hampton. For years, this sandstone house, considered a
> **white elephant** with its fifteen bedrooms, indoor pool,
> and imported Italian frescoes, had stood vacant.
>
> — Candace Bushnell, *Trading Up*, 2003

The white elephant, a rare whitish or light-gray form of the Asian elephant, is regarded with special veneration in regions of Southeast Asia and India. According to some Buddhist scriptures, Queen Maya conceived the Buddha while dreaming of a white elephant entering her womb. It is said that in Siam (what is now Thailand), the king would honor a member of his court by presenting him with a white elephant together with land and the means to feed and support the animal. It was strictly forbidden to put a white elephant to work lifting logs and performing other tasks like an ordinary elephant.

If the king wanted to get rid of a member of his court who had displeased him however, he presented a white elephant to be maintained at the courtier's own expense. The courtier could hardly refuse the king's generosity, nor could he pass the elephant along to someone else, so the royal gift usually resulted in the courtier's financial ruin.

In the 19th century, it was probably the popularity of such stories that led people to use the term *white elephant* to describe a burdensome possession or unprofitable piece of property. Still later, the expression came to be used of any article that is simply of no use to its owner.

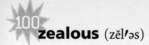

zealous (zĕl′əs)

adjective

Passionately devoted to a cause, ideal, or goal.

> For all its secular posturing, science has in common with many religions a **zealous** adherence to the concept of sin. There are the deadly scientific sins, like fabricating results or failing to give proper credit to one's peers; and there are the little sins, like experimental sloppiness or appearing once too often on television.
>
> — Natalie Angier, *The Beauty of the Beastly*, 1995

> When the Reds won the World Series exactly half a century ago, their **zealous** fans mobbed Fountain Square and dismantled a nearby trolley car. When giddy Cincinnatians returned to the scene of the 1940 crime Saturday night — actually, this morning — to celebrate the fifth world championship in Reds history, they didn't so much as tug the tail on one of the horses that pull carriages around the square. In fact, the fans were so orderly that they actually swept up after themselves.
>
> — Lonnie Wheeler, "Waiting Game for Fans," *New York Times*, October 22, 1990

[From Medieval Latin *zēlōsus*, from *zēlus*, zeal, from Greek *zēlos*.]

The 100 Words

accolade
acrimony
angst
anomaly
antidote
avant-garde
baroque
bona fide
boondoggle
bourgeois
bravado
brogue
brusque
byzantine
cacophony
camaraderie
capricious
carte blanche
Catch-22
caustic
charisma
cloying
déjà vu
dichotomy
dilettante
disheveled
élan
ennui
epitome
equanimity
equivocate
esoteric
euphemism
fait accompli

fastidious
faux pas
fiasco
finagle
Freudian slip
glib
gregarious
harbinger
hedonist
heresy
idiosyncratic
idyllic
indelicate
infinitesimal
insidious
junket
kitsch
litany
lurid
Machiavellian
malaise
malinger
mantra
maudlin
mercenary
minimalist
misnomer
narcissist
nirvana
non sequitur
nouveau riche
oblivion
ogle
ostentatious

ostracize
panacea
paradox
peevish
perfunctory
philistine
precocious
propriety
quid pro quo
quintessential
red herring
revel
rhetoric
scintillating
spartan
stigma
stoic
suave
Svengali
sycophant
teetotaler
tête-à-tête
tirade
tryst
ubiquitous
unrequited
untenable
vicarious
vile
waft
white elephant
zealous